Get America Singing...Again!

Strategies for Teaching

Lesson Ideas and Activities for Meeting the Standards

By Loretta Mitchell Norgon

To Russell Lepisto – my father – with gratitude and love

HAL•LEONARD®
CORPORATION
7777 W. BLUEMOUND RD. P.O. BOX 13819 MILWAUKEE, WI 53213

Preface

Music educators once envisioned a common repertoire, a collection of songs that every student should know and be able to sing. The collection of songs, ***Get America Singing…AGAIN*** is the result of a national effort to revive singing, not only with our students, but in communities across the country. The Get America Singing…Again! campaign established a common song repertoire that "Americans of all ages, know and can sing," a diverse, well-researched collection of songs to promote and revive community singing.

Along with that dream, came another – the vision of a resource combining our common song repertoire with teaching strategies to meet the National Standards. This publication, ***Strategies for Teaching (Set A)***, makes that vision a reality, synthesizing the song collection with classroom teaching strategies.

Strategies for Teaching (Set A) contains ready-to-use ideas for integrating essential repertoire into our everyday teaching. With these activities, we can work toward and achieve the National Standards – what every student should know and be able to do in music. This resource becomes the missing link between our common singing repertoire and achievement of the National Standards.

The book contains ten sections, one for each of ten songs from ***Get America Singing…AGAIN Volume I***. Each section features teaching ideas and learning activities, aligned specifically with one or more of the National Standards. The strategies are designed to integrate seamlessly with national as well as local music standards.

Created for music specialists and classroom teachers of Grades K through 8, each activity targets one or more grade levels. The reproducible pages can be duplicated to create transparencies or individual student copies. Student learning activities such as "About the Song," "Learning the Lyrics," "Create an Arrangement," and "Adding Orff," help students interact with the song material as they work toward the Standards.

Teacher instructions are designed to be user-friendly, providing the information that music teachers need most quickly and concisely. Each includes:

Grade Level(s):
National Standard(s)
Objective(s):
Materials:
Directions:

Use all of the ideas, or pick and choose those learning activities which fit the needs of your curriculum, your classroom and/or your own teaching style. Feel free to adapt, modify, and extend. You may wish to modify the difficulty level of some activities to meet the needs of students older or younger than those for whom the activity was intended. The suggestions may further serve as a springboard for your own ideas – your own creative ways of using use our common song repertoire for standards-based instruction.

I hope that this resource will help you incorporate America's favorite songs into your classroom as you help your students meet the National Standards.

Loretta Mitchell Norgon

Get America Singing...Again!

Strategies for Teaching (Set A)

Lesson Ideas and Activities for Meeting the Standards

Battle Hymn of the Republic

Activity 1-1: Show the Steady Beat

Grade Level: 1-2
National Standard: 2

Objective

Students feel and play the steady beat.

Materials

- Get America Singing…AGAIN! Singer's Edition, p. 10
- Transparency and Student copies of 1-1
- Classroom rhythm instruments

Directions

Display transparency. As students sing the refrain, demonstrate the steady beat by touching each flag on the transparency. Invite a student to show the steady beat , using the transparency. Distribute student copies of 1-1. Invite students to touch each flag as they feel the steady beat. Collect the student copies. Distribute classroom rhythm instruments and help students follow the transparency, playing the steady beat - once for each flag symbol - as they sing the refrain.

Activity 1-2: Play Along

Grade Level: 1-2
National Standard: 2

Objective

Students play easy melodic patterns on mallet instruments or keyboards.

Materials

- Get America Singing…AGAIN! Singer's Edition, p. 10
- Transparency or student copies of 1-2
- Mallet instruments or keyboards

Directions

Display the transparency or distribute student copies of 1-2. Help students read the icons and match them to the melody. Select individual students to play the melody fragment. Sing the refrain with the class. Invite individuals to play along. Add the verse, singing it as a solo. Invite the class and the bell (keyboard) players to join in on the refrain.

Activity 1-3: About the Song

Grade Level: 3-4

National Standard: 9

Objective

Students understand the origin and background of songs in their varied repertoire.

Materials

- Get America Singing…AGAIN! Singer's Edition, p. 10
- Student copies of 1-3
- Pencils

Directions

Open the class period by singing the chorus. Ask, "How many of you have heard this song before?" Facilitate a class discussion including any of the following:

- Where students have heard this tune
- What lyrics they recall
- What meaning they attach to the song
- What other lyrics they have heard or sung that go with this melody

Distribute student copies of 1-3: About the Song. Invite students to read individually or as a class as appropriate to students' reading abilities. Facilitate a class discussion using the "Questions for Discussion."

Activity 1-4: Learn the Lyrics

Grade Level: 3-4

National Standard: 1

Objective

Students sing a song from memory.

Materials

- Get America Singing…AGAIN! Singer's Edition, p. 10
- Student copies of 1-4
- Pencils

Directions

Open the class period by singing the verse and refrain. Distribute Singers Editions and student copies of 1-4. Invite students to complete the page, working individually, as partners, or as a class as appropriate to students' reading abilities. Challenge students to sing the verse from memory.

Activity 1-5: Study Guide

Grade Level: 5-8

National Standard: 9

Objective

Students understand the origin and background of songs in their varied repertoire.

Materials

- Get America Singing...AGAIN! Singer's Edition, p. 10
- Student copies of 1-5
- Pencils

Directions

Distribute student copies of 1-5. Invite students to read the background information individually or as a class. Divide students into groups. Instruct groups to complete the Vocabulary Builder exercise as instructed on the student page.

Possible student responses: activitst - a worker for a political cause; woman's suffrage - the right for women to vote; clergyman - ordained minister of the church; lyrics - the words of a song; melody - pitches arranged as a musical idea; verse - a section or part of a song; published - made available (in print) to the public; composing - creating or "making up" as original; anonymously - name withheld.

Activity 1-6: Singing Harmony

Grade Level: 5-8

National Standard: 1

Objective

Students sing music written in two parts.

Materials

- Get America Singing...AGAIN! Singer's Edition, p. 10
- Student copies of 1-6

Directions

Distribute student copies of 1-6. As students are able to maintain the melody, introduce and rehearse the harmony. Divide the class into two groups. Sing the refrain along with the harmony part. Sing the entire song - verses in unison, and the refrain with harmony. Allow groups to reverse parts and sing the song again.

Activity 1-7: Show What You Know
Grade Level: 5-8
National Standard: 9

Objective
Students understand the origin and background of songs in their varied repertoire.

Materials
- Get America Singing…AGAIN! Singer's Edition, p. 10
- Student copies of 1-7
- Pencils

Directions
Distribute student copies of 1-7. Instruct students to work individually, in partners, or in small groups. Debrief the activity by encouraging students to share their responses with the class.

Battle Hymn of the Republic

Show the Steady Beat

Directions: Sing the refrain and touch the flags to show the steady beat

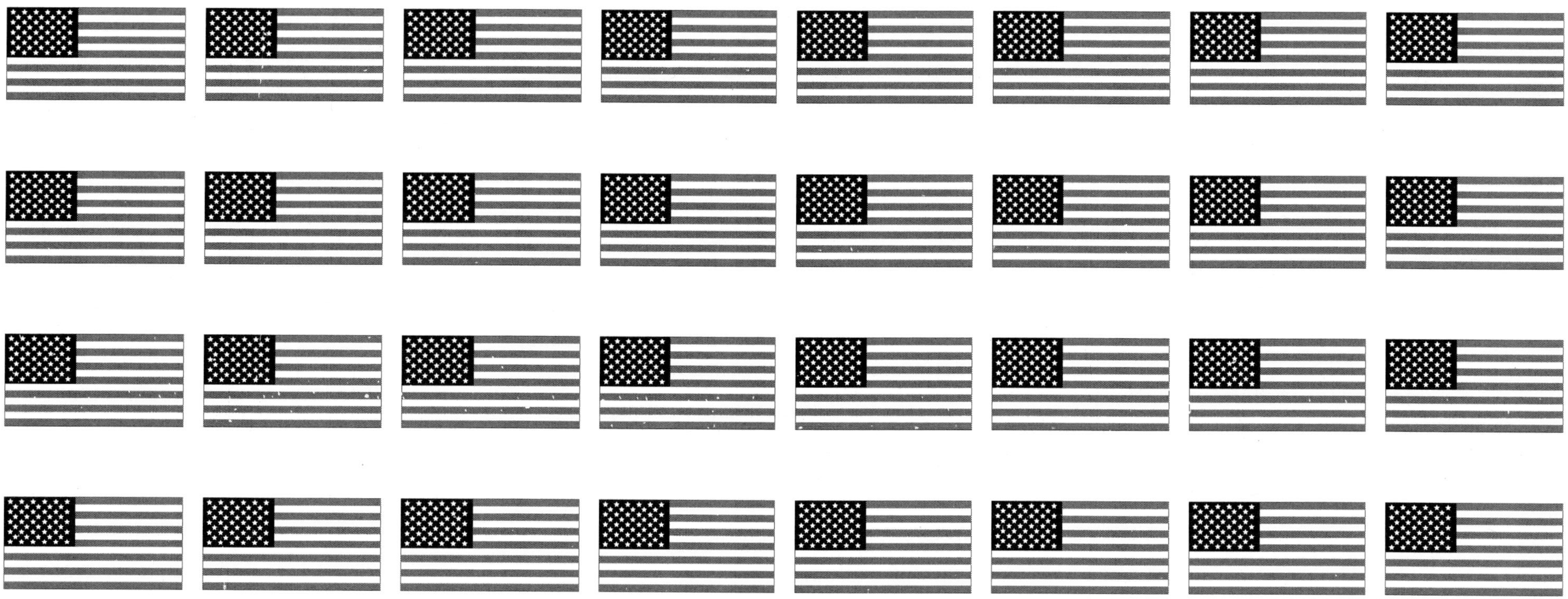

Battle Hymn of the Republic

Play Along

Find these bells. Play along with the song.

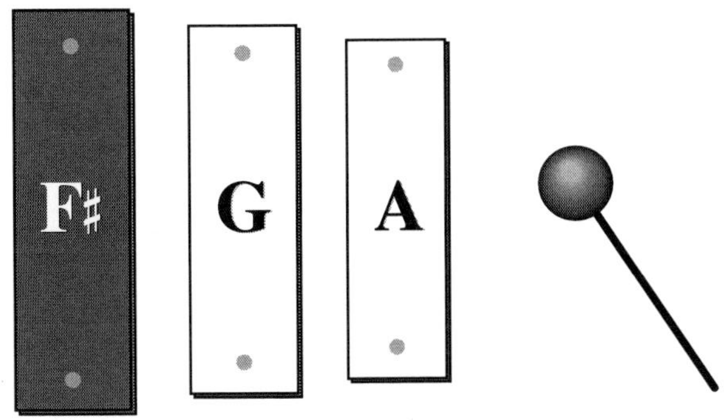

G	A	A	G	F♯	G
His	truth	is	march-	ing	on—

Battle Hymn of the Republic

About the Song

It was the time of the Civil War. A woman named Julia Ward Howe heard soldiers singing "John Brown's Body," as they were marching.

Mrs. Howe wanted to write new words for the melody. One night, she was not able to sleep. She rose from her bed and wrote two verses. She finished other verses later. A magazine printed her poem and paid her $5.00 for her work.

A man named William Steffe composed the tune that inspired Mrs. Ward to write this poem. The tune has been used with many other lyrics.

"Battle Hymn of the Republic" is a favorite to many Americans. It is called a patriotic song because it expresses feelings of pride about our country.

Questions for Discussion

1. What other words have you heard with this melody?

2. What other patriotic songs do you know?

3. Why do people like to sing songs about their feelings for their country?

4. Do other countries have patriotic songs?

Battle Hymn of the Republic

Learn the Lyrics

Directions: Fill in the missing words to complete verse one of this famous patriotic song.

Mine ________________ have seen the

______________ of the ________________

of the ______________.

He is ____________________ out the

________________ where the ______________

of ______________ are stored.

He hath ____________ the fateful ____________

of His terrible swift _________________.

His ______________ is __________________ on.

Choose from these words:

loos'd	wrath
glory	trampling
vintage	lightening
truth	coming
marching	Lord
sword	eyes
grapes	

Battle Hymn of the Republic

Study Guide

Background Information

During the time of the Civil War, Julia Ward Howe, an activist for womens' suffrage, attended a military parade. She and her husband heard the marching tune "John Brown's Body," a war song sung by troops returning to Washington.

At the suggestion of her clergyman, Mrs. Howe began to compose a new set of lyrics to the melody. That night, having difficulty sleeping, she rose from her bed to complete a verse or two, afraid that she may forget them if she slept through the night.

Her poem was published in the *Atlantic Monthly*, in February 1862. She was paid $5.00 for her work and the poem was published anonymously.

A man named William Steffe, is most often given credit for composing the melody. The tune has been used for many other songs, including "John Brown's Body" and "Say, Brothers, Will You Meet Us?"

The melody is frequently heard combined with lyrics other than Julia Ward Howe's poem. What other versions have you heard?

Vocabulary Builder

What do these words and phrases mean? Discuss these terms with your group. Look up the ones you do not know. Agree on a definition for each term and write it in the blank.

activist ______________________________

woman's suffrage ______________________________

clergyman ______________________________

lyrics ______________________________

melody ______________________________

verse ______________________________

published ______________________________

composing ______________________________

anonymously ______________________________

Battle Hymn of the Republic
Singing Harmony

Lyrics by Julia Ward Howe
Music by William Steffe
Harmony Part by Loretta Norgon

Refrain

Battle Hymn of the Republic

Show What You Know

Name______________________________ Class__________ Date________

Write your answers to the following questions:

1. Retell the story about how this poem was written.

____

____

____

____

____

2. What did you find interesting about this story?

____

____

____

3. What words in the poem tell you that it was written during a time of war?

____

____

____

____

4. Choose three of the following Vocabulary Builder words or phrases. Write a paragraph using the terms you choose.

Civil War	activist	woman's suffrage	military
clergyman	lyrics	melody	verse
published	composing	anonymously	trampling
vintage	grapes of wrath		

____

____

____

____

____

____

____

____

Do-Re-Mi

Activity 2-1: Climb the Stairs

Grade Level: K-1

National Standards: 1, 5

Objectives

Students sing a song from memory.
Students use a system (syllables) to read pitch notation.

Materials

- Get America Singing…AGAIN! Singer's Edition, p. 14
- Transparency and Student copies of 2-1
- Pencils, crayons, or fine point markers

Directions

Display transparency. Point to each illustration to help students learn the lyrics. Use the stairs to illustrate the use of the solfege syllables in this song. Invite a student to point as the group sings. Distribute student copies of 2-1. Instruct students to follow their maps as they sing the song. Invite students to draw self-portraits in the space provided.

Activity 2-2: Play the Scale

Grade Level: K-2

National Standard: 2, 5

Objectives

Students play easy melodic patterns on mallet instruments or keyboards.
Students use a system (syllables) to read pitch notation.

Materials

- Get America Singing…AGAIN! Singer's Edition, p. 14
- Transparency and Student copies of 2-2
- Mallet instruments or keyboards

Directions

Display the transparency. Help students read the map and demonstrate by playing each pitch of the major scale as it begins a phrase in the song. Select individual students to play the major scale on mallet instruments or keyboards. Sing the song with the class as selected students play along. As students become familiar with the song and are ready, distribute instruments to every student along with student copies of 2-2. Allow guided practice, assisting individuals as needed.

Activity 2-3: Improvise on Do Re Mi

Grade Level: 2-3

National Standard: 3

Objective

Students improvise short songs and instrumental pieces

Materials

- Teacher copy of 2-3
- Transparency of 2-2
- Resonators bells: C, D, E or Orff mallet instrument with other bars removed
- Mallets

Directions

Make sure that students have prerequisite skills necessary to improvise successfully (e.g., mallet technique, starting and ending on time, keeping a steady beat, playing with an accompaniment, etc.) Display transparency of 2-2. Circle or highlight Do, Re, and Mi on the illustration. To students: "You will be improvising today, using only these three pitches: Do, Re, and Mi." Play the accompaniment provided on 2-3 (or improvise a suitable accompaniment, 16 beats in length).* Invite students to take turns improvising sixteen-beat DoReMi melodies.

*Recommendation: Computer sequencing applications make it possible to record, save, and play back the accompaniment. Utilizing technology in this way, prior to class time, frees the teacher to work directly with students and assist them during the class period.

Activities: 2-4: Getting Creative
2-5: Our Do Re Mi Composition

Grade Level: 2-3

National Standard: 4

Objective

Students create short instrumental pieces within specified guidelines.

Materials

- Student copies of 2-4
- Student copies and transparency of 2-5
- Scissors
- Resonators bells: C, D, E or Orff mallet instrument with other bars removed
- Mallets
- (Optional) Teacher copy of 2-3

Directions

Using cards cut from two copies of 2-4, demonstrate procedures and learning strategies to the large group. Illustrate how to sequence 12 of the Do Re Mi cards into four 4-beat phrases, each containing the rhythm pattern ta ta ta-ah (quarter, quarter, half note). With the class, sing and play the composition which results. (Remind students that the final phrase should end on the home tone- Do.) Invite students to comment and revise. Sing the revised composition. Continue until students understand the procedure. Record the "finished" composition on the transparency (2-5) and perform. Divide students into small groups. Distribute 2 copies of 2-4 and mallet instruments to each group. Instruct students to cut Do Re Mi cards apart, sort like cards into six piles, and begin to create Do Re Mi melodies. Remind students to sing and play as they work, revising until the group agrees on the composition. Distribute copies of 2-5 to each group, and instruct groups to record their final product on the page. Invite groups to perform their compositions for the whole class. (Optional) Using 2-3 or teacher-created accompaniment, encourage groups to perform their compositions with accompaniment.

Activity 2-6: Read and Play

Grade Level: 3-4

National Standard: 2, 5

Objectives

Students play easy melodic patterns on mallet instruments or keyboards

Students use a system (syllables) to read pitch notation.

Materials

- Get America Singing...AGAIN! Singer's Edition, p. 14
- Transparency and student copies of 2-6
- Mallet instruments or keyboards

Directions

Display the transparency. Help students read the map and demonstrate by playing one sustained pitch for each pitch of the major scale as it begins each phrase in the song. Select individual students to play the major scale on bells or keyboards. Sing the song with the class as selected students play along. As students are ready, distribute individual instruments and student copies of 2-6. Allow guided practice, assisting individuals as needed.

Activities 2-7: What's Cooking?
2-8: Recipe Cards

Grade Level: 3-4
National Standard: 4

Objective

Given a rhythm pattern, students create a melody.

Materials

- Student copies and transparencies of 2-7 and 2-8
- Resonators bells: C, D, E, G, A or Orff mallet instruments with other bars removed

Directions

Display transparencies of 2-7 and 2-8. Using class input, demonstrate how to read the prescribed rhythm pattern and use the "ingredients" on the pitch recipe card to create an instrumental piece. (Remind students that the final phrase should end on the home tone - Do.) Record the "finished" composition on the 2-7 transparency and sing. Divide students into small groups. Distribute student copies and instruments to each group. Instruct students to create their own melodies. Remind them to sing and play as they work, revising until the group agrees on the composition. Invite groups to perform their compositions for the class.

Activity 2-9: Study Guide

Grade Level: 5-8
National Standard: 9

Objective

Students understand the origin and background of songs in their varied repertoire.

Materials

- Get America Singing...AGAIN! Singer's Edition, p. 14
- Student copies of 2-9
- Pencils

Directions

Distribute student copies of 2-9. Invite students to read the background information individually or as a class. Discuss the suggested research projects. Encourage students to suggest other ideas to continue their study of the song and the musical. Assign research projects for individuals, partners, or groups, along with specific requirements of the assignment.

Possible student responses: Richard Rodgers - composer, wrote the music; Oscar Hammerstein II - librettist/lyricist, wrote the text or words; Lindsay and Crouse - wrote the play; Julie Andrews - starred in the movie version as Fraulein Maria; Christopher Plummer - starred in the movie version as Captain von Trapp

Activity 2-10: A Classic Musical

Grade Level: 5-8
National Standard: 9

Objective

Students understand the origin and background of songs in their varied repertoire.

Materials

- Get America Singing...AGAIN! Singer's Edition, p. 14
- Student copies of 2-10
- Pencils
- Recording of *The Sound of Music* soundtrack
- Videotape of film version *The Sound of Music*

Directions

Distribute student copies of 2-10. As individuals, partners, small groups, or entire class, use 2-10 to launch a research project to study the songs from the musical *The Sound of Music*.

Who sings?

The Sound of Music: Maria

Do-Re-Mi: Maria and the von Trapp children

Edelweiss: Captain von Trapp

Lonely Goatherd: Maria and the von Trapp children

Climb Every Mountain: Mother Abbess

My Favorite Things: Maria and the von Trapp children

Musical characteristics:

For all songs: student responses will vary, based on student backgrounds in musical analysis.

Activity 2-11: Show What You Know

Grade Level: 5-8
National Standard: 1, 9

Objective

Students understand the origin and background of songs in their varied repertoire.

Materials

- Student copies of 2-11
- Pencils

Directions

Distribute student copies of 2-11. Instruct students to work individually, in partners, or in small groups. Debrief the activity by encouraging students to share their responses with the class.

Do-Re-Mi

Climb the Stairs

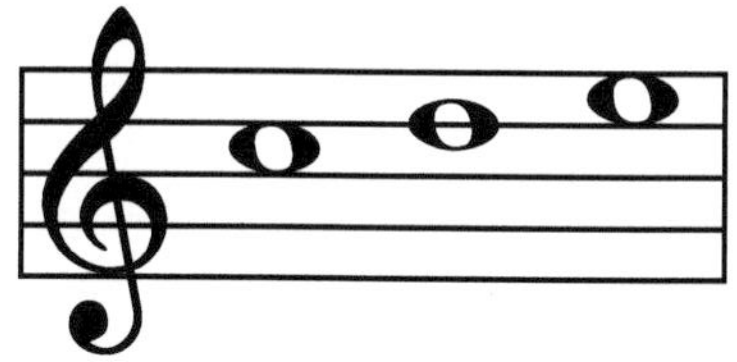

Draw a picture of yourself in the frame.

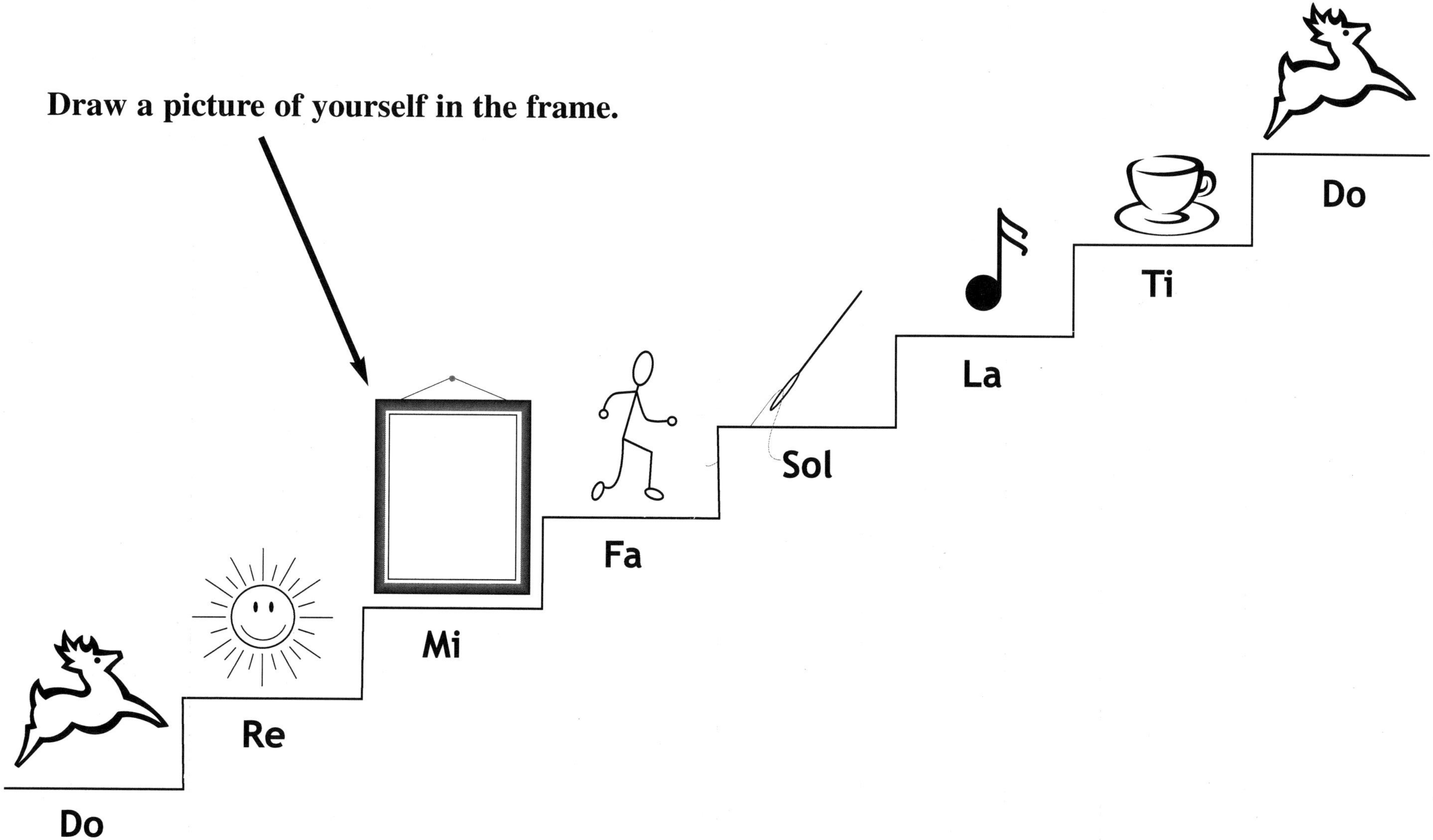

Do-Re-Mi

Play the Scale

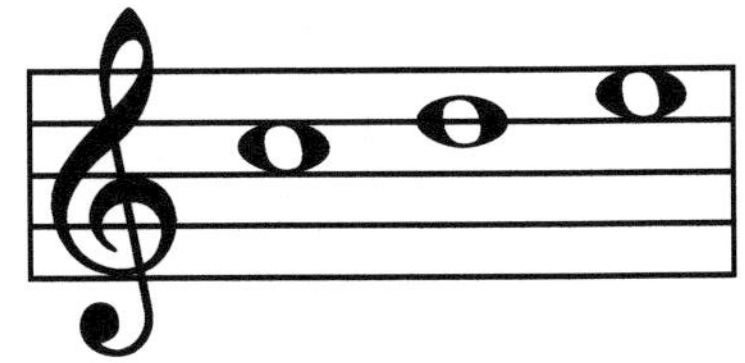

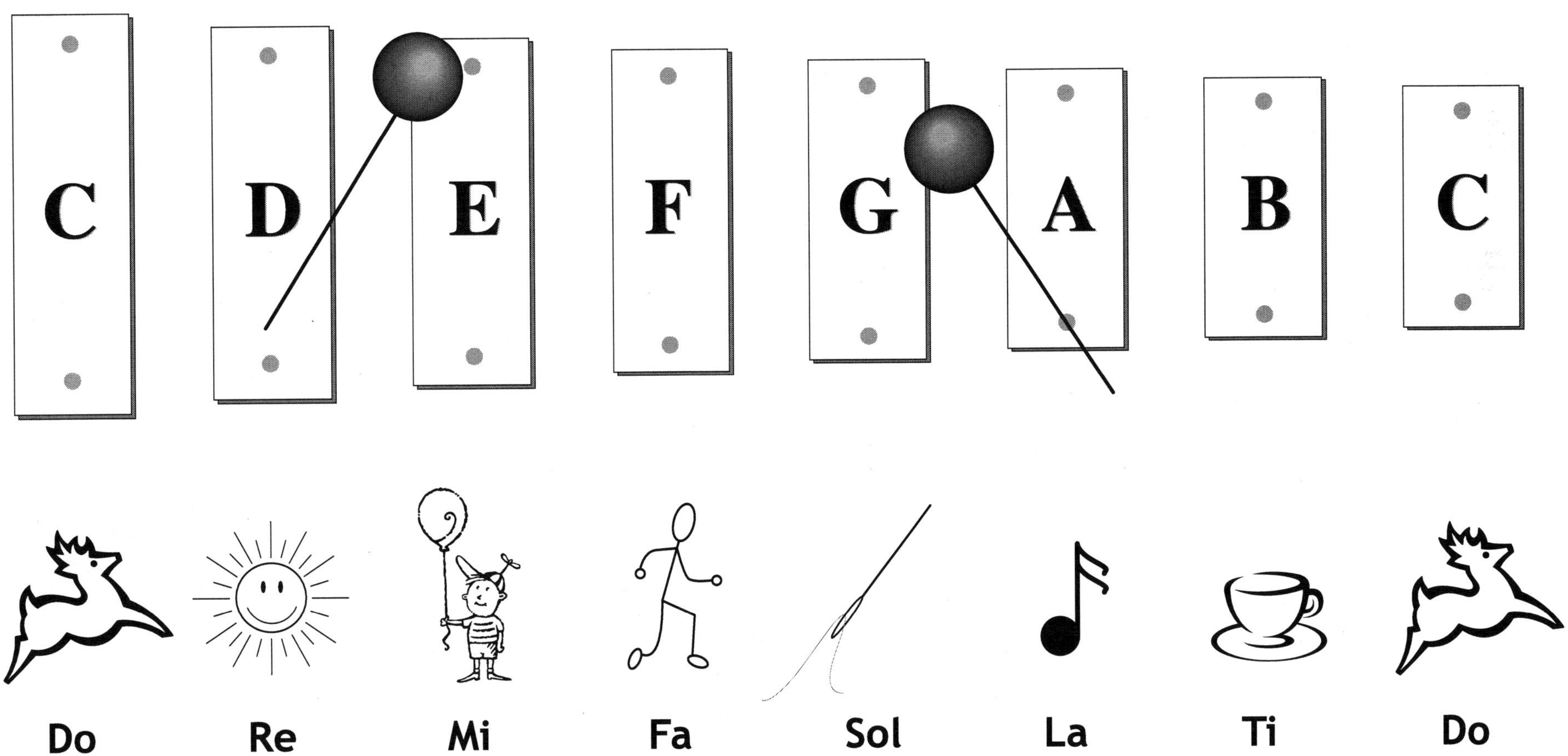

Do-Re-Mi

Improvise on Do-Re-Mi

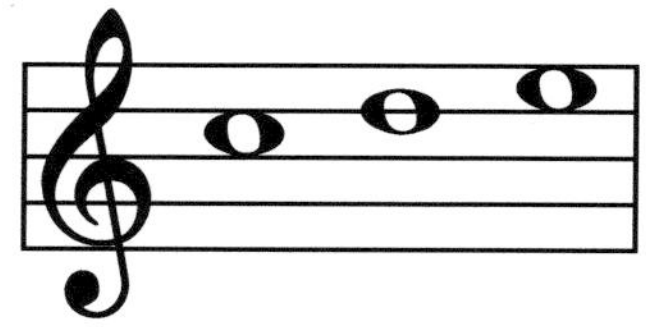

Keyboard Accompaniment by Loretta Norgon

Do-Re-Mi

Getting Creative

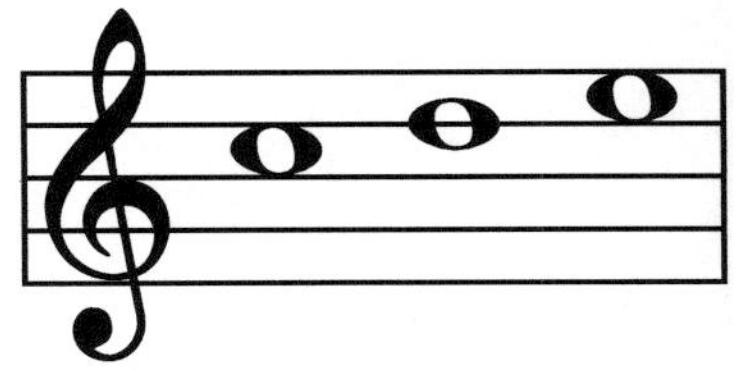

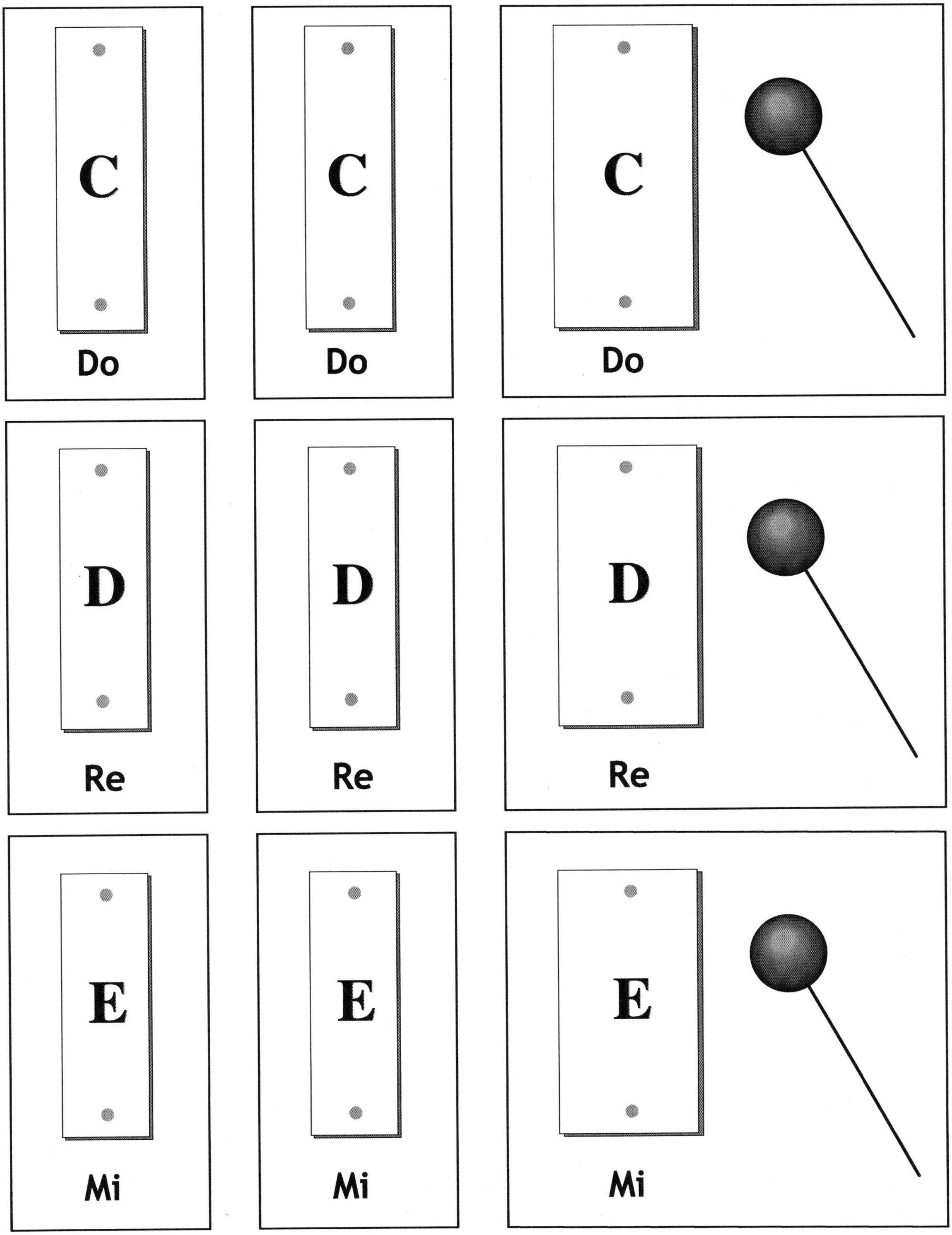

Do-Re-Mi

Our Do Re Mi Composition

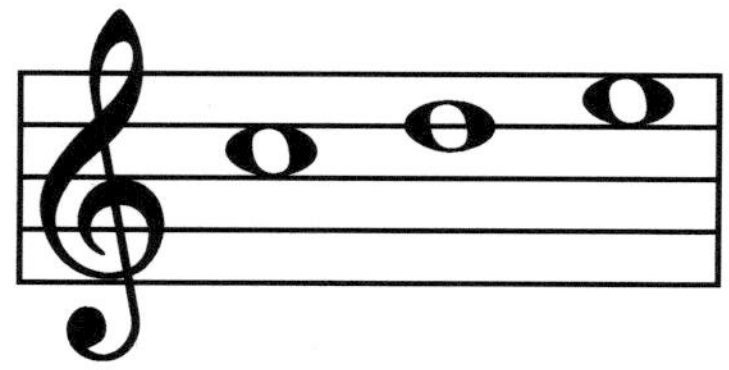

Group Members: ____

____

Do-Re-Mi

Read and Play

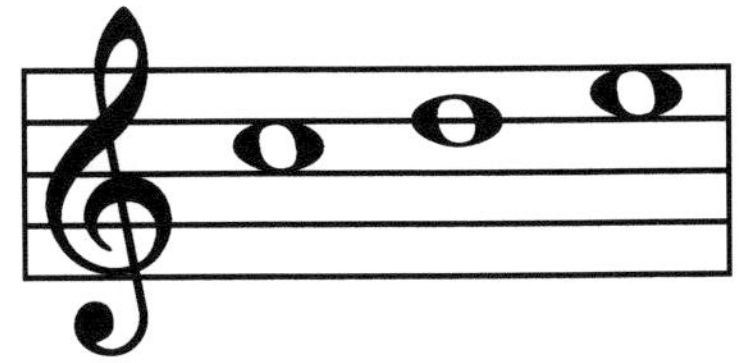

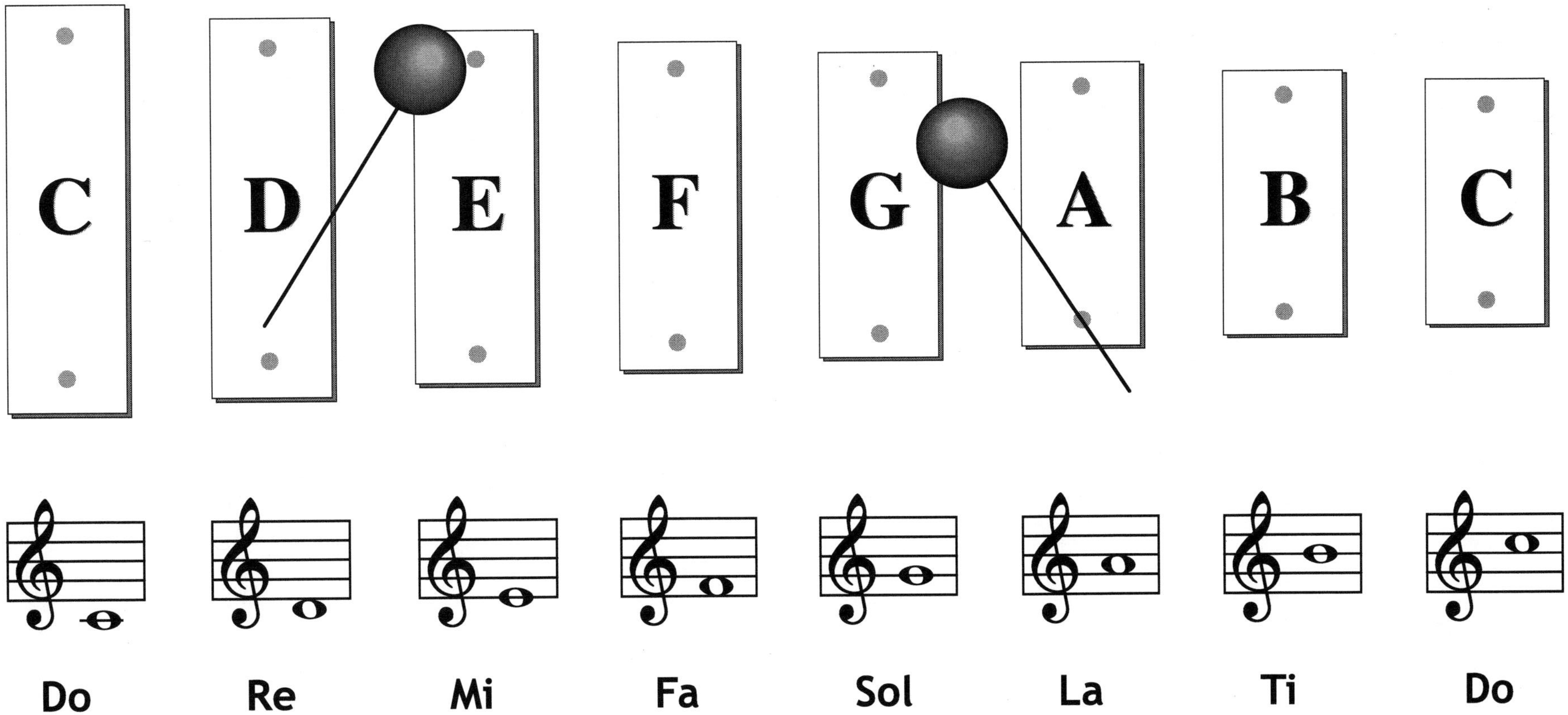

Do-Re-Mi

What's Cooking?

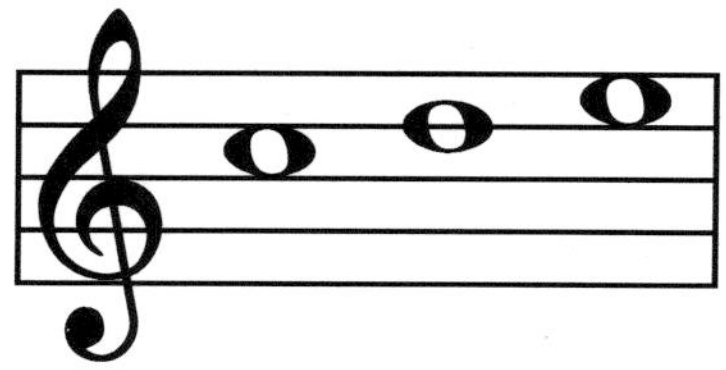

Directions:
1. Use the pitches and rhythms on the recipe cards.
2. Experiment with your ingredients.
3. Write your pirches in the spaces below.

4. Play your song.
5. Make any changes and try it again.
6. Play your song for the class.

Do-Re-Mi

Recipe Cards

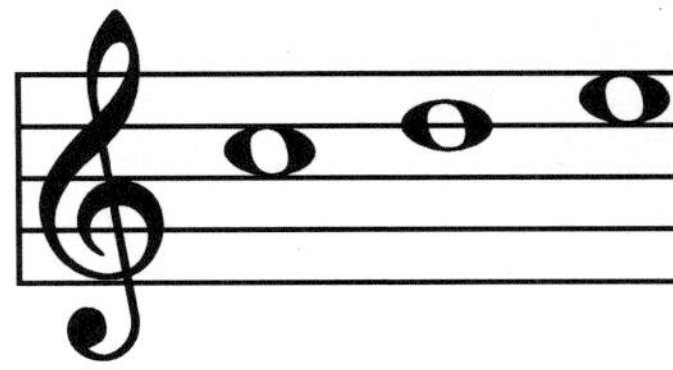

1. Choose from these "ingredients" for the pitches of your song.

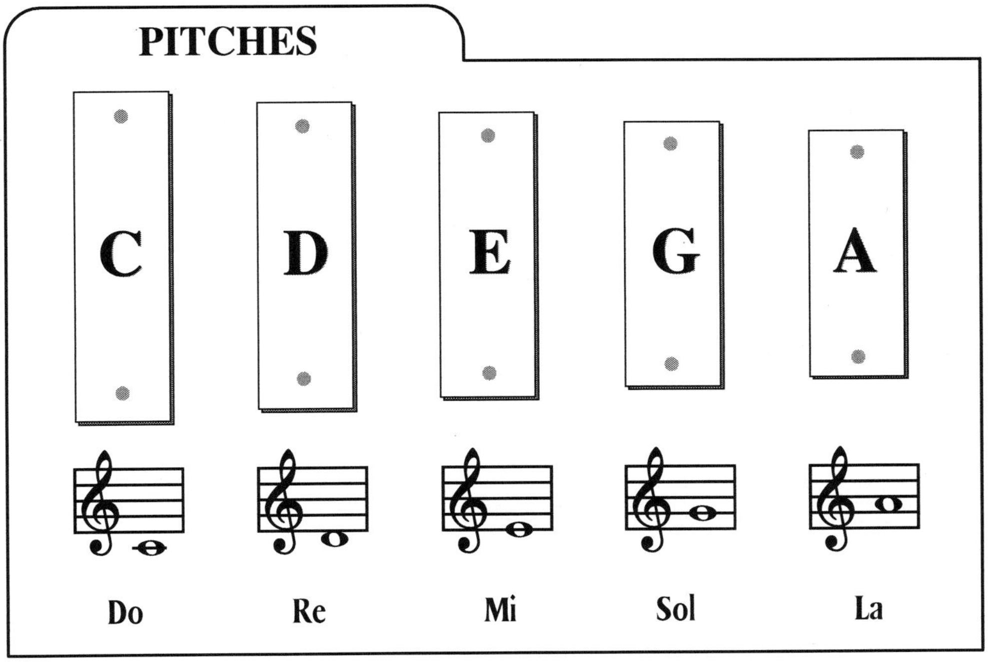

2. Use these "ingredients" for the rhythm of your song.

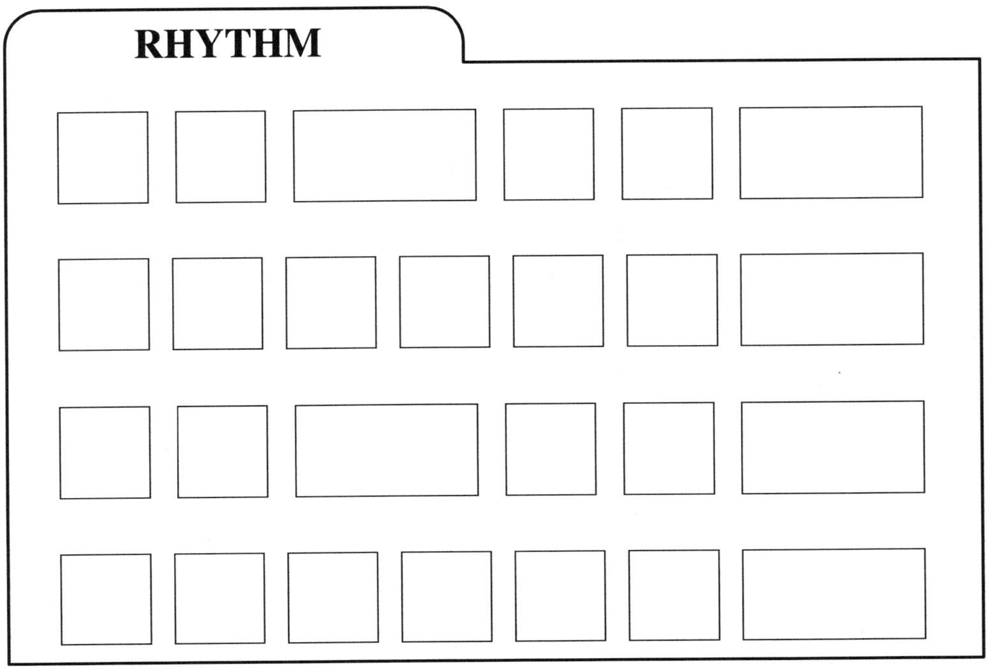

Rodgers and Hammerstein

Study Guide

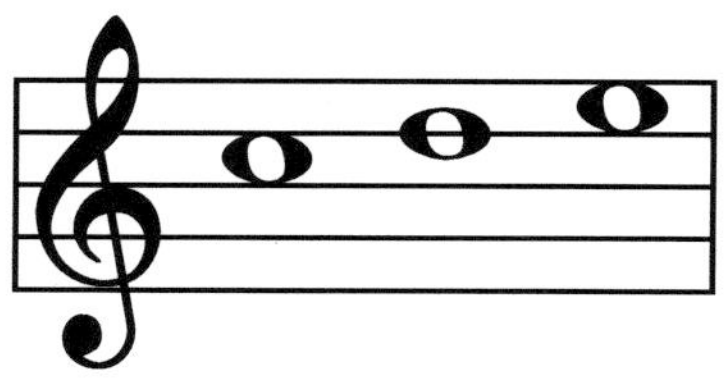

Richard Rodgers and Oscar Hammerstein II

One of the most famous teams in American musical theater, Richard Rodgers and Oscar Hammerstein II collaborated to produce titles such as *Oklahoma*, *Carousel*, *South Pacific*, *The King and I*, and *The Sound of Music*. Rodgers was the composer of the team and Hammerstein wrote the lyrics for their musicals. Together, they earned Academy Awards, Tony Awards, Grammy Awards, and Emmy Awards.

The Sound of Music

Set in Austria in the late 1930s, *The Sound of Music* is the true story of a young postulant, named Maria, who is sent to serve as a governess for the seven children of Captain Von Trapp, a widowed naval officer. The children and their father fall in love with Maria, and she and the captain are married. Returning from their honeymoon, they discover that the Nazis have invaded Austria and have demanded that the Captain take a commission in the Nazi Navy. The family flees from Austria, escaping by foot over the mountains to Switzerland.

The musical premiered on Broadway in 1959. The film version was released in 1965, and won five Academy Awards. Songs by Rodgers and Hammerstein included "The Sound of Music," "Climb Every Mountain," "My Favorite Things," Edelweiss," and "Do Re Mi."

Do-Re-Mi

Maria, the governess, uses the song, "Do-Re-Mi" to teach the seven Von Trapp children about the "ingredients of music" and how notes can be put together to create millions of songs. The children begin singing together, and even perform as a singing group, the Von Trapp Family Singers.

Research Projects

1. Who were the following, and what were their connections to the movie, *The Sound of Music*.

   Richard Rodgers — Oscar Hammerstein II — Lindsay and Crouse
   Julie Andrews — Christopher Plummer

2. Can you find a recording of Maria and the Von Trapp children singing "Do-Re-Mi?"
3. Ask a member of your family what they recall about this movie.
4. *The Sound of Music* was nominated for ten Oscars. What were they?
5. Identify the following:

   Academy Award — Tony Award — Grammy Award — Emmy Award

The Sound of Music

A Classic Musical

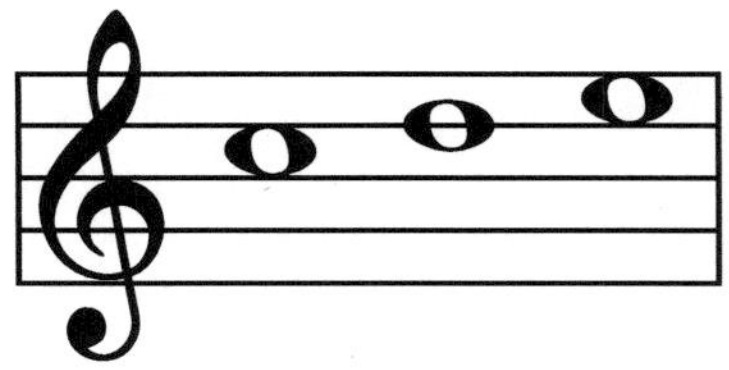

Directions: Do-Re-Mi is one of many well-known songs from the classic musical *The Sound of Music*. Oscar Hammerstein II wrote the lyrics and Richard Rodgers composed the music. Find out more about the other songs from this musical. Do some research and fill in the chart below.

Song Title	Who sings this song?	Musical Characteristics
The Sound of Music		
Do-Re-Mi		
Edelweiss		
Lonely Goatherd		
Climb Every Mountain		
My Favorite Things		

The Sound of Music

Show What You Know

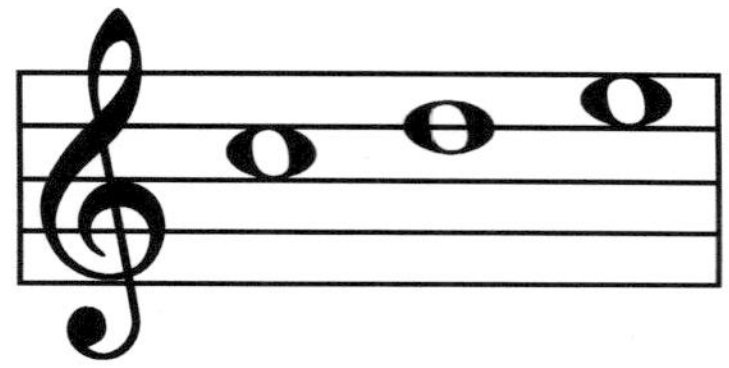

Name______________________________ Class__________ Date_________

Write your answers to the following questions:

1. Write something interesting that you learned about the team of Richard Rodgers and Oscar Hammerstein II.

2. Write a paragraph describing the story of the musical, *The Sound of Music*.

3. Why was this musical so successful?

4. Choose one song from the musical and describe its musical characteristics.

Frère Jacques

Activity 3-1: New Lyrics

Grade Level: K-2
National Standards: 4

Objective

Students create new lyrics for a familiar melody.

Materials

- Get America Singing…AGAIN! Singer's Edition, p. 16
- Transparency of 3-1

Directions

Display transparency*. Help students read the "starter lines" for a new song. Use student suggestions to finish the song. Rehearse and perform the new version. Encourage students to make suggestions for revision and try it again. Once the class agrees, publish copies for all students to take home and perform for their families.

*Teacher may wish to enlarge one section of transparency, to display only one of the four choices for students to use.

Activity 3-2: Learn the Signs

Grade Level: K-4
National Standard: 8

Objective

Students perform a song with signs.

Materials

- Get America Singing…AGAIN! Singer's Edition, p. 16
- Transparency of 3-2

Directions

Display the transparency. Introduce and demonstrate signs one at a time. Allow time for students to practice each sign, reviewing and incorporating the previously learned signs as new ones are added. Perform the song with the signs.

Activity 3-3: Add an Ostinato

Grade Level: 2-3

National Standard: 2

Objective
Students perform ostinati.

Materials
- Get America Singing…AGAIN! Singer's Edition, p. 16
- Transparency of 3-3
- Resonators bells: E flat and low B flat

Directions
Display transparency of 3-3. Guide students to perform ostinatos by speaking, singing, and playing. Add ostinati to the song.

Activity 3-4: A New Ostinato

Grade Level: 2-4

National Standards: 1, 5

Objective
Students read and sing ostinati.

Materials
- Get America Singing…AGAIN! Singer's Edition, p. 16
- Transparency of 3-4

Directions
Display transparency. With students, choose an ostinato to add to the song. Read and rehearse the ostinato. Divide class into two groups, and assign the ostinato to one group and the song to the other. Reverse parts and sing the song again. As time permits, choose another ostinato to add to the song. Add more than one ostinato to create a more complex harmonic texture.

Activity 3-5: Adding Orff

Grade Level: 2-4

National Standard: 2, 4, (5)

Objectives

- Students perform simple instrumental parts while other students sing or play contrasting parts.
- (Optional) Students read traditional notation in 4/4 meter.
- Students create an arrangement.

Materials

- Get America Singing…AGAIN! Singer's Edition, p. 16
- Teacher copy or transparency of 3-5

Directions

Note transposition to Key of F. Teach instrumental parts to students by reading or by rote. With student input, create an arrangement, layering instrumental parts to create a complex and interesting texture.

Activity 3-6: Around the World

Grade Level: 3-4

National Standard: 8

Objective

Students sing a song in several world languages.

Materials

- Get America Singing…AGAIN! Singer's Edition, p. 16
- Transparency and student copies of 3-6
- Mallet instruments or keyboards

Directions

Display the transparency. Help students choose a language and conduct research to learn to pronounce the words, first speaking and then singing. Use the internet, the media center, and resource people or volunteers to assist with research and pronunciation. Choose another language and repeat the process.

Activity 3-7: Add a Partner Song

Grade Level: 3-4

National Standard: 1

Objective

Students sing partner songs.

Materials

- Get America Singing…AGAIN! Singer's Edition, p. 16
- Student copies of 3-7

Directions

Note transposition to Key of D major. Distribute student copies of 3-7. As students are able to maintain the melody, introduce and rehearse "Three Blind Mice." Divide the class into two groups. Sing "Frère Jacques" with the partner song. Allow groups to reverse parts and sing the partner songs again.

Activity 3-8: Mahler's Symphony No. 1 in D Major "Titan"

Grade Level: 3-8

National Standard: 6

Objective

Students identify and describe events in a listening example.

Materials

- Student copies and transparency of 3-8: Mahler's Symphony No. 1 in D Major "Titan"
- Recording of Mahler's Symphony No. 1 in D Major, Third Movement

Directions

Use 3-8 as a teaching aid to help students follow the musical events in Mahler's Symphony. Focus specifically on Mahler's use of the "Frère Jacques" motive (in minor), and his use of imitation. Encourage students to answer the questions, and describe events as they occur.

Activity 3-9: More Translations
Grade Level: 5-8
National Standard: 8

Objective
Students research translations of a song.

Materials
- Get America Singing…AGAIN! Singer's Edition, p. 16
- Student copies of 3-9
- Pencils

Directions
Distribute student copies of 3-9. Discuss the research project. Assign research project for individuals, partners, or groups, along with specific requirements of the assignment. Invite students to share their research with the class, reading or performing the song in other languages.

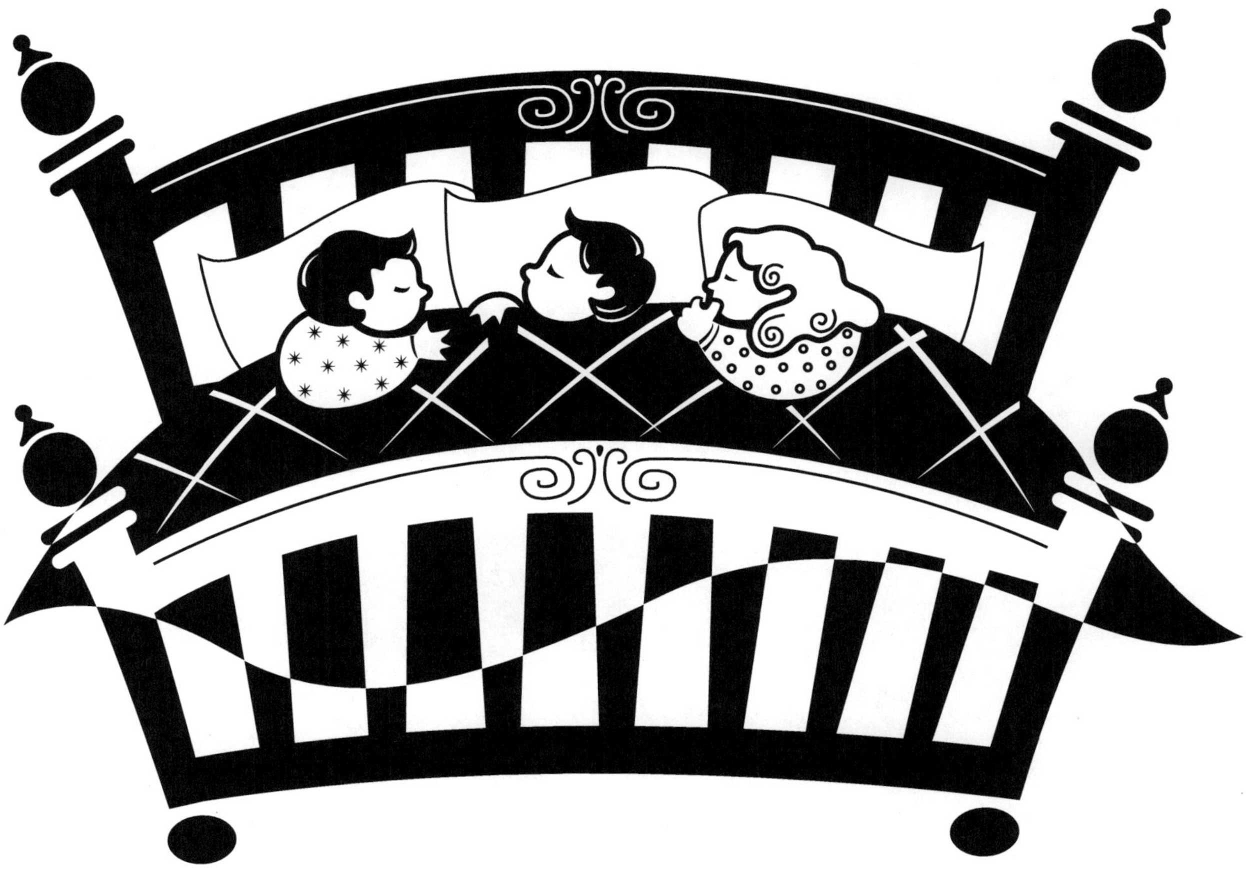

Frère Jacques

New Lyrics

Ride the school bus,
Ride the school bus,
Ev'ry day.
Ev'ry day.

I like first grade,
I like first grade,
So do you.
So do you.

Pledge allegiance
Pledge allegiance
To the flag
To the flag

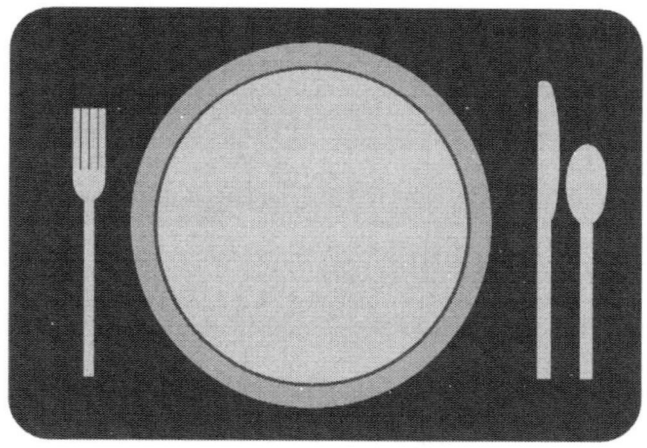

Where's the menu?
Where's the menu?
What's for lunch?
What's for lunch?

Frère Jacques

Learn the Signs

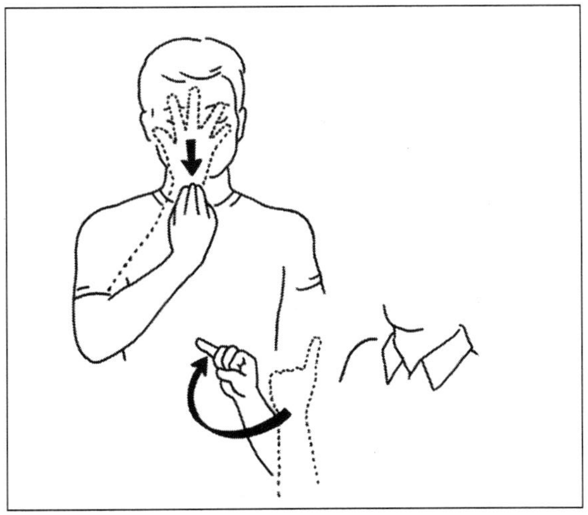

sleeping

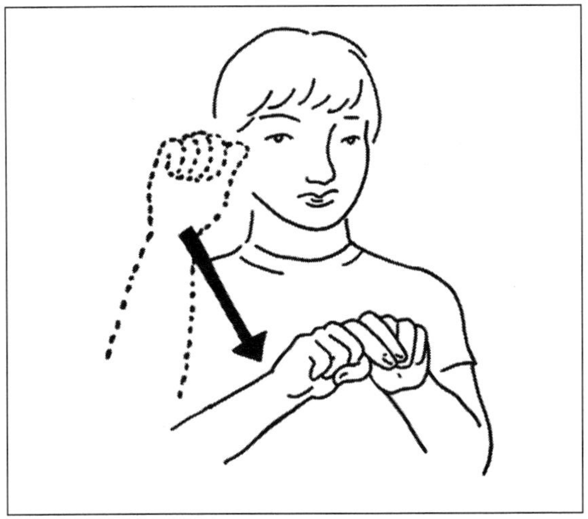

brother

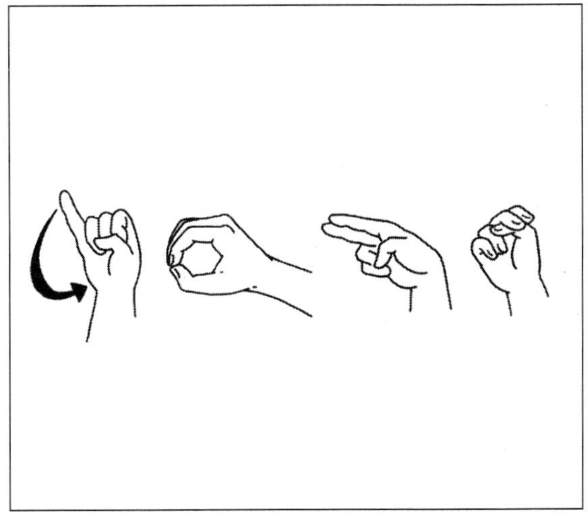

John

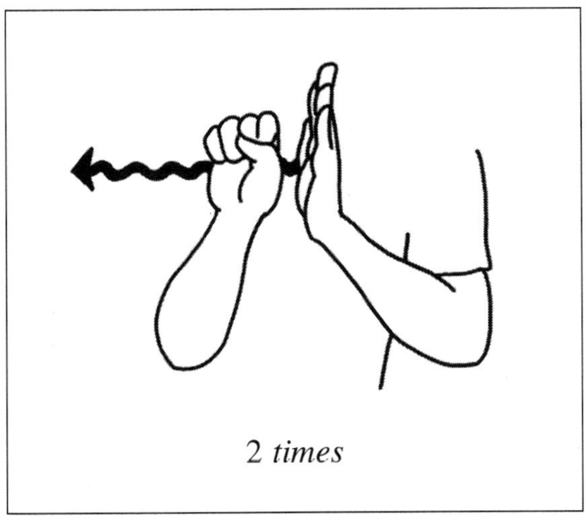

bells

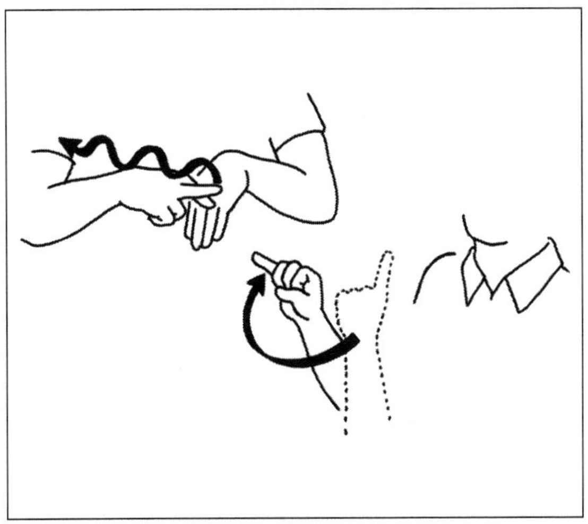

ringing

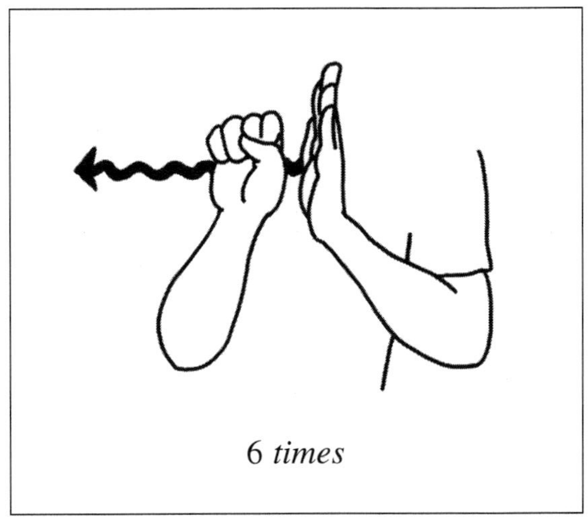

ding dong

Frère Jacques

Add an Ostinato

Speak an ostinato.

Ding **Ding** **Dong**

Sing an ostinato.

Ding **Dong**

Ding

Play an ostinato.

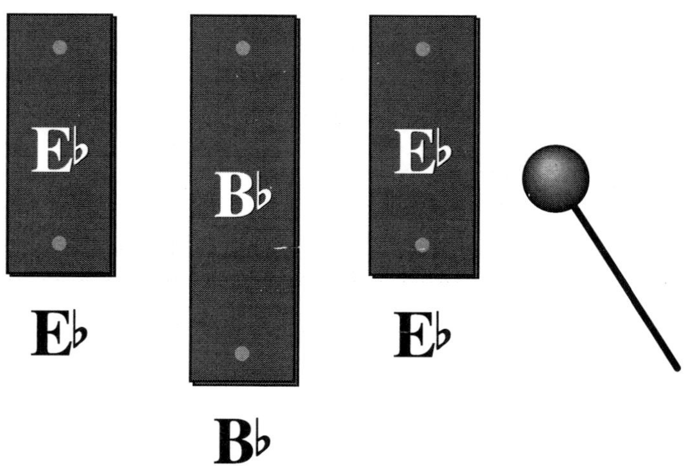

Frère Jacques

A New Ostinato

Ostinato Activity by Loretta Norgon

1

2

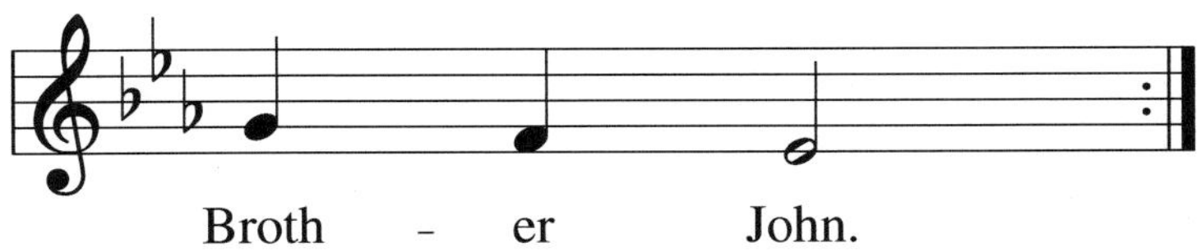

3

4

5

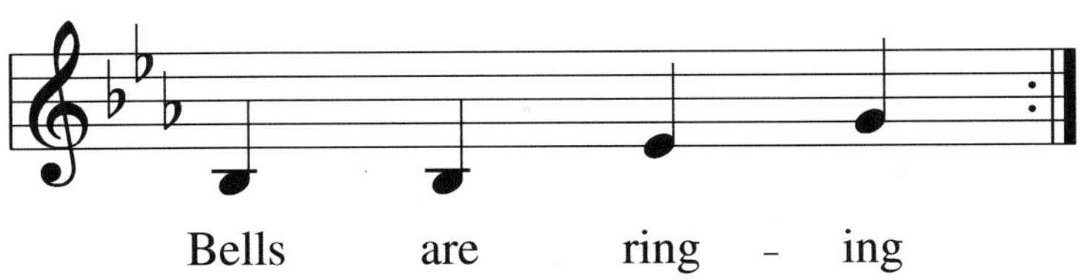

Frère Jacques
Adding Orff

SG = Soprano Glockenspiel
SX = Soprano Xylophone
AX = Alto Xylophone
SR = Soprano Recorder
BX = Bass Xylophone
BM = Bass Metallophone

French Round
Arranged by Loretta Norgon

Frère Jacques

Around the World

Spain

Martinillo, Martinillo,
¿dónde estás?
¿dónde estás?
Suenan las campanas.
Suenan las campanas.
Ding dang dong
Ding dang dong

Italy

Fra Martino
Campanero,
Duermes ya?
Duermes ya?
Suena la campana,
Suena la campana.
Din don dan,
Din don dan.

China

Iiang zhi lao hu,
Iiang zhi lao hu
pao de kuai
pao de kuai
yi zhi mei you er duo
yi zhi mei you wei ba
hen qi guai
hen qi guai

France

Frère Jacques,
Frère Jacques,
Dormez-vous?
Dormez-vous?
Sonnez les matines,
Sonnez les matines.
Din din don,
Din din don.

Finland

Jaako kulta
Jaako kulta
Herää jo?
Herää jo?
Kellojasi soita,
Kellojasi soita.
Ding ding dong.
Ding ding dong.

Germany

Bruder Jakob,
Bruder Jakob,
Schläfst du noch?
Schläfst du noch?
Hörst du nicht die Klocken?
Hörst du nicht die Klocken?
Ding dang dong.
Ding dang dong.

Frère Jacques
Add a Partner Song

Frère Jacques

Mahler's Symphony No. 1 in D Major "Titan"

Third Movement

A

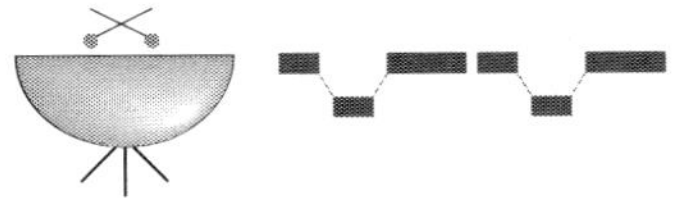

Listen for the round

B

What other instruments do you hear?

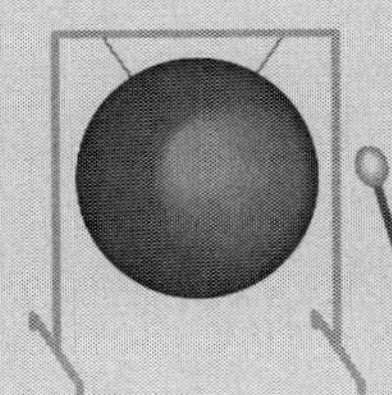

Listen for the round

A[1]

What is different from A?

How does it end?

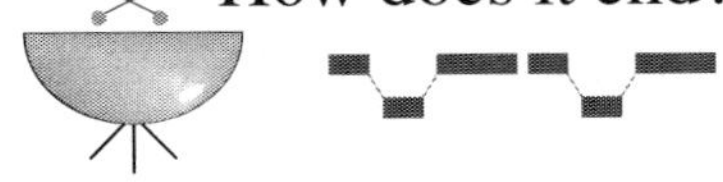

Frère Jacques

More Translations

Directions: Use the internet or any other resource to find translations of this song in other languages. Find a pronunciation guide and learn to sing the song in the languages you find.

Lanugage: ____________________

Lyrics:

Lanugage: ____________________

Lyrics:

Lanugage: ____________________

Lyrics:

Lanugage: ____________________

Lyrics:

I've Been Working on the Railroad

Activity 4-1: Picture Map

Grade Level: K-2

National Standards: 1

Objective

Students sing a song from memory.

Materials

- Get America Singing...AGAIN! Singer's Edition, p. 24
- Transparency and student copies of 4-1

Directions

Display transparency. Help students use the illustrations as they learn the lyrics and melody of the song. Distribute student copies. Assist students as they follow their own copies of the map and sing the song. Encourage students to take their copies home and perform the song for their families.

Activity 4-2: Play Along

Grade Level: 2-3

National Standard: 2

Objective

Students perform easy melodic patterns on bells or keyboards.

Materials

- Get America Singing...AGAIN! Singer's Edition, p. 24
- Transparency and Student copies of 4-2
- Mallet instruments or keyboards

Directions

Display the transparency or distribute student copies of 4-2. Help students read the icons and match them to the melody. Select individual students to play the melody. Sing the beginning of the song with the class. Invite individuals to play along. Perform the entire song. Select other students to play as the class sings.

Activity 4-3: About the Song

Grade Level: 3-4
National Standard: 9

Objective

Students understand the origin and background of songs in their varied repertoire.

Materials

- Get America Singing…AGAIN! Singer's Edition, p. 24
- Student copies of 4-3
- Pencils

Directions

Distribute student copies of 4-3. Invite students to read the background information individually or as a class. Divide students into groups. Direct groups to complete the Vocabulary Builder exercise as suggested on the student page.

Activity 4-4: Learn the Lyrics

Grade Level: 3-4
National Standard: 1

Objective

Students sing a song from memory.

Materials

- Get America Singing…AGAIN! Singer's Edition, p. 24
- Student copies of 4-4
- Pencils

Directions

Distribute Singers Editions and student copies of 4-4. Begin by singing the song. Invite students to complete the page, working individually, as partners, or as a class, as appropriate to students' reading abilities. Challenge students to sing the verse from memory.

Activity 4-5: Complete the Map

Grade Level: 3-4
National Standard: 1

Objective
Students sing a song from memory.

Materials
- Get America Singing...AGAIN! Singer's Edition, p. 24
- Transparency and student copies of 4-5
- Pencils

Directions
Distribute Singers Editions and student copies of 4-5. Begin by singing the song. Invite students to analyze and then follow the sections of the map. Challenge students to create icons to represent the lyric and musical content of the remaining two sections.

Activity 4-6: Add a Descant

Grade Level: 5-8
National Standard: 1

Objective
Students sing music written in two parts.

Materials
- Get America Singing...AGAIN! Singer's Edition, p. 24
- Student copies of 4-6

Directions
Distribute student copies of 4-6. As students are able to maintain the melody, introduce and rehearse the descant. Divide the class into two groups. Sing the song with the descant. Allow groups to reverse parts and sing the song again.

Activity 4-7: Working on the Lyrics
Grade Level: 5-8
National Standard: 9

Objective
Students understand the origin and background of songs in their varied repertoire.

Materials
- Get America Singing…AGAIN! Singer's Edition, p. 24
- Transparency of 4-7

Directions
Distribute student copies of 4-7. Instruct students to follow the directions, working individually, in partners, or in small groups. Debrief the activity by encouraging students to share their lyrics with the class. (This activity builds on Activity 4-3 from earlier grade levels.)

I've Been Working on the Railroad

Picture Map

I've been working on the railroad

Dinah, won't you blow?

Someone's in the kitchen with Dinah

I've Been Working on the Railroad

Play Along

Directions: Find these bells. Play along with the song.

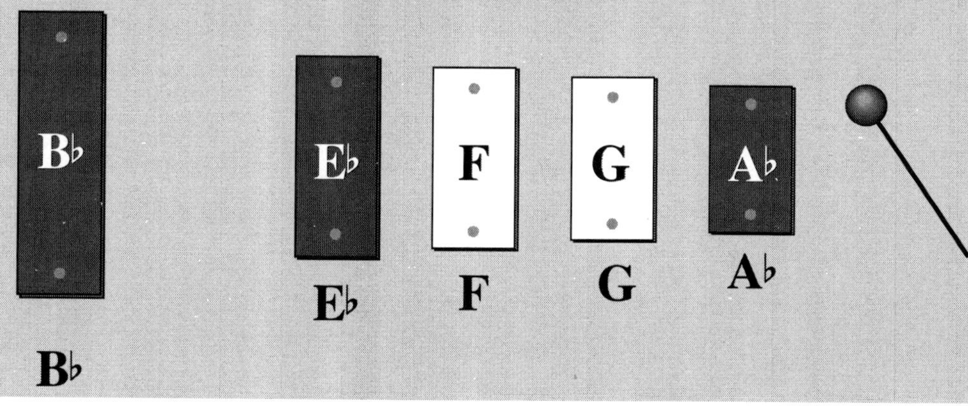

E♭	B♭					G	E♭	A♭		E♭		G
I've	been	work-	ing	on	the	rail	road	All	the	live-	long	day.

I've Been Working on the Railroad

About the Song

The growth of a system of railroads was a very important part of America's history. With rail travel, Americans began to travel and ship their cargo by train, relying less and less on traveling by horseback, stagecoach, or on foot.

The origin of the song, "I've Been Working on the Railroad" is somewhat unclear. No one person is credited as the composer. The song probably appeared with an earlier title, "The Levee Song," with lyrics about working, not on the railroad, but on the levee.

After the Civil War, railroad workers probably sang the chorus of "The Levee Song" with modified lyrics about railroads, as they labored during the long work day.

The tune is also used with another set of lyrics. Perhaps you have heard the song, "The Eyes of Texas Are Upon You."

Vocabulary Builder

What do these words and phrases mean? Discuss these terms with your group. Look up the ones you do not know. Agree on a definition for each term and write it in the blank.

stagecoach ______________________________

cargo ______________________________

origin ______________________________

composer ______________________________

Civil War ______________________________

levee ______________________________

labored ______________________________

I've Been Working on the Railroad

Learn the Lyrics

Directions: Fill in the missing words

I've been working on the ________________ all

the livelong ________________. I've been

________________ on the railroad, just to

________________ the ________________ of

________________. Can't you ________________ the

________________ blowin'? ________________ up

so ________________ in the ________________.

Can't you hear the ________________ shoutin',

"________________, blow your horn?"

Choose from these words:

day	hear
working	captain
morn	pass
whistle	time
Dinah	day
early	Rise
railroad	

I've Been Working on the Railroad

Complete the Map

I've been working on the railroad

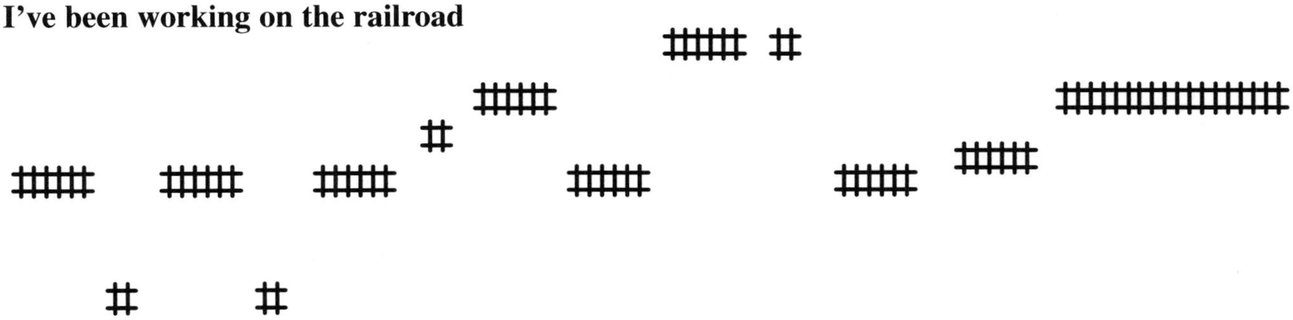

Dinah, won't you blow?

Someone's in the kitchen with Dinah

Fee-fi-fid-dle-ee-i-o

I've Been Working on the Railroad

Add a Descant

Traditional
Descant by Loretta Norgon

I've Been Working on the Railroad

Working on the Lyrics

Name______________________________ Class_________ Date________

I've Been Working on the Railroad

I've been working on the railroad
All the live long day
I've been working on the railroad
Just to pass the time away.
Can't you hear the whistle blowin'?
Rise up so early in the morn.
Can't you hear the captain shoutin',
"Dinah, blow your horn?"

I've Been Working on the Levee

I've been working on the levee
All the live long day
I've been working on the levee
Just to pass the time away.
Can't you hear the whistle blowin'?
Rise up so early in the morn.
Can't you hear the captain shoutin',
"Dinah, blow your horn?"

Write your answers to the following questions:

1. What is the origin of the song "I've Been Working on the Railroad?"

____

____

____

2. Compare the lyrics of the song with the lyrics of the "Levee Song."

____

____

____

3. What words in the lyrics may signal that lunch time is near?

____

____

____

4. Compose your own lyrics for this song. Begin with the lyrics that are printed below. Add your own ideas to complete an original version of this song. Sing your song using the tune for "I've Been Working on the Railroad."

I've Been Working

Lyrics by ____________________

I've been working ____________________

____

____

____

____

____

____

____

____

Teacher Instructions

Dona Nobis Pacem

Activity 5-1: About the Song

Grade Level: 3-4
National Standards: 8, 9

Objectives

Students understand the origin and background of songs in their varied repertoire.
Students identify ways which music is connected to other disciplines (Latin language).

Materials

- Get America Singing...AGAIN! Singer's Edition, p. 30
- Transparency and student copies of 5-1

Directions

Distribute student copies of 5-1. Invite students to read individually or as a class as appropriate to students' reading abilities. Divide students into groups. Instruct groups to confer, using the "Questions for Discussion." Select a representative from each group to report on the group's discussion and answers to the questions.

Activity 5-2: Adding Orff

Grade Level: 3-4
National Standard: 2, 4, (5)

Objectives

- Students perform simple instrumental parts while other students sing or play contrasting parts.
- (Optional) Students read traditional notation in 3/4 meter.

Materials

- Get America Singing...AGAIN! Singer's Edition, p. 30
- Teacher copy or transparency of 5-2

Directions

Note transposition to Key of F Major. Teach instrumental parts to students by reading or by rote. With student input, create an arrangement, layering instrumental parts to create a complex and interesting texture.

Activity 5-3: Recorder Duet

Grade Level: 3-4

National Standard: 2, 5

Objectives

- Students perform independent instrumental parts while other student play contrasting parts.
- Students read half, quarter, eighth, and dotted notes and rests in a 3/4 meter signature.

Materials

- Get America Singing…AGAIN! Singer's Edition, p. 30
- Student copies of 5-3

Directions

Note transposition to Key of G Major. Distribute student copies of 5-3. Divide class into two groups. Assist one group in learning to play the melody. Assist the other group in learning to play the harmony part. Pair each student with a partner from the opposite group, and allow time for the partners to rehearse their duets. Encourage duets to perform for the class. Reassemble the original groups, and work with each group to help them learn the opposite part. Pair with partners again. Allow time for practice, and performances.

Activity 5-4: Singing Harmony

Grade Level: 5-8

National Standard: 1

Objective

Students sing music written in two or more parts.

Materials

- Get America Singing…AGAIN! Singer's Edition, p. 30
- Transparency and student copies of 5-4

Directions

Distribute student copies of 5-4. As students are able to maintain the melody, sing the song in a two-part and then a three-part round with entrance as indicated. Introduce and rehearse the first countermelody. Divide the class into two groups. Sing the song with the countermelody. When students are ready, help them learn the other countermelody, and then the bass line. Combine any or all of the harmony components to create a complex and interesting harmonic texture.

Activity 5-5: Create an Arrangement

Grade Level: 5-8

National Standard: 4

Objective

Students arrange a simple piece for voices or instruments.

Materials

- Get America Singing…AGAIN! Singer's Edition, p 30
- Student copies of 5-5

Directions

Distribute student copies of 5-5. Divide students into groups, and instruct them to follow directions as printed to create an arrangement of the song. Allow time for groups to create and practice their arrangements. Invite groups to volunteer to perform their arrangements for the teacher or for the class.

Activity 5-6: Create a New Harmony Part

Grade Level: 5-8

National Standard: 1, 4

Objective

Students create and sing a harmony part.

Materials

- Get America Singing…AGAIN! Singer's Edition, p 30
- Student copies of 5-6

Directions

Distribute student copies of 5-6. Divide students into groups, and instruct them to create a harmony part, choosing from the pitches indicated above each measure. Allow time for groups to create and then practice their harmony parts. Encourage them to sing the harmony part with the melody of "Dona Nobis Pacem." Play the accompaniment as printed, or create an original accompaniment. Invite groups to perform their harmony parts for the teacher or for the class.

Activity 5-7: Show What You Know

Grade Level: 5-8

National Standard: 9

Objective

Students understand the origin and background of songs in their varied repertoire.

Materials

- Get America Singing...AGAIN! Singer's Edition, p. 30
- Student copies of 5-8
- Pencils

Directions

Distribute student copies of 5-7. Instruct students to work individually, in partners, or in small groups. Encourage students to share their responses with the class. (This activity builds on Activity 5-1 from earlier grade levels.)

Dona Nobis Pacem

About the Song

The song "Dona Nobis Pacem" has been sung in many parts of the world for hundreds of years. It is probably from the 16th century! It was originally intended to be sung as a canon.

Latin	Pronunciation	English
Dona	do - nah	give
Nobis	no - bihs	us
Pacem	pah - chem	peace

The words, can be translated quite easily. "Dona" (from which we get the English word "donate," means "give." "Nobis" means "us." "Pacem" is the root of our English words "pacify," "pact," and "peace."

So, the words of this song can be translated as "Give us peace." Sung over and over in a canon or round, the message is repeated and made very clear.

Questions for Discussion

1. What is the origin of this song?

2. What do the lyrics mean?

3. What other Latin words and phrases do you know?

4. What is a canon?

Dona Nobis Pacem
Adding Orff

SG = Soprano Glockenspiel
SX = Soprano Xylophone
AX = Alto Xylophone
SR = Soprano Recorder
BX = Bass Xylophone
BM = Bass Metallophone

Arranged by Loretta Norgon

Dona Nobis Pacem

Adding Orff

Arranged by Loretta Norgon

Dona Nobis Pacem
Recorder Duet

Recorder Arrangement by
Loretta Norgon

Dona Nobis Pacem

Singing Harmony

Harmony Activity by Loretta Norgon

1. Sing as a round.

2. Add a countermelody.

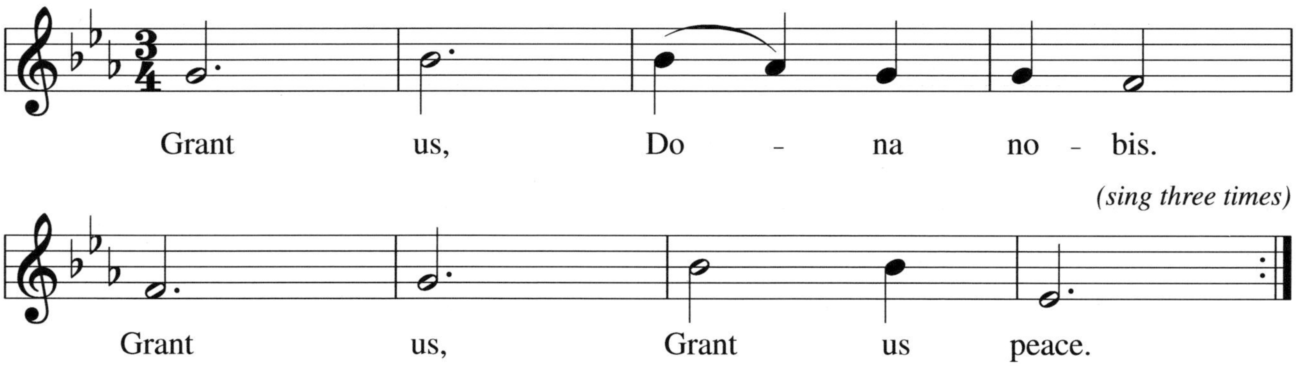

3. Add another countermelody.

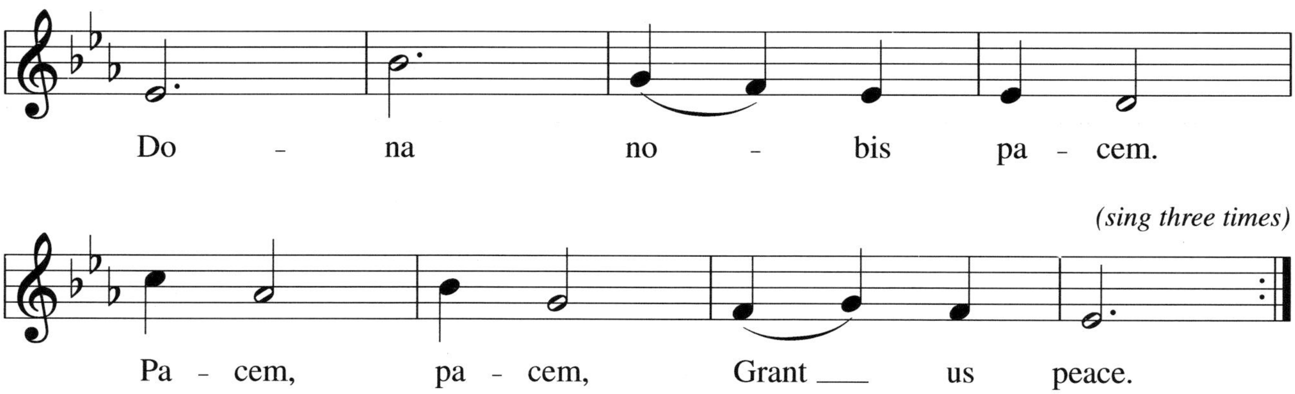

4. Add a bass line.

5. Divide your class into several groups, and combine them all.

Dona Nobis Pacem

Create an Arrangement

Class: ____________________

Date: ____________________

Group members: ____

Directions: With your group, create an arrangement of the song "Dona Nobis Pacem." Follow the steps below.

Step 1

Consider all the possibilities. Use this list to get started. Add to the list.

Latin lyrics	Bass Line	____________
Introduction	Round	____________
Coda	Speaking Voices	____________
Add instruments	Electronic sound sources	____________
Countermelody		

Step 2

Choose from your list the items you'd like to include in your arrangement. List your items in the blanks below. You do not need to fill all the blanks. Your group can decide how many items to use. Also, you may use an item more than once, or in combination with another item.

____________ ____________ ____________ ____________

____________ ____________ ____________ ____________

____________ ____________ ____________ ____________

Step 3

Rearrange your list so that your items are in the order you'd like them to occur. Use the "Special Information" space to add notes about who will perform, the dynamics you choose, or other information. You do not need to use all of the blanks. You may add more blanks if needed.

1. ____________ Special Information: ______________________________
2. ____________ Special Information: ______________________________
3. ____________ Special Information: ______________________________
4. ____________ Special Information: ______________________________
5. ____________ Special Information: ______________________________
6. ____________ Special Information: ______________________________
7. ____________ Special Information: ______________________________
8. ____________ Special Information: ______________________________
9. ____________ Special Information: ______________________________
10. ____________ Special Information: ______________________________

Step 4

Try your arrangement. Revise anyting that you'd like to change. Try it again. When it's finished, practice until you're ready to perform for your teacher. Maybe you'd like to perform you arrangement for your class!

Dona Nobis Pacem
Create a New Harmony Part

Harmony Activity by Loretta Norgon

Dona Nobis Pacem

Show What You Know

Name________________________________ Class__________ Date________

Dona nobis pacem, pacem
Dona nobis pacem
Dona nobis pacem
Dona nobis pacem
Dona nobis pacem
Dona nobis pacem

Write your answers to the following questions:

1. What do the lyrics of this song mean?

____

____

____

2. If you were going to compose music to fit these words, how would your song sound?

____

____

____

____

3. Explain the following terms:

countermelody_______________________________________

duet _______________________________________

descant_______________________________________

canon _______________________________________

round _______________________________________

harmony _______________________________________

compose _______________________________________

Music Alone Shall Live

Activity 6-1: Playing the Chord Roots

Grade Level: 3-4

National Standards: 2

Objective

Students play chord roots to accompany a song.

Materials

- Get America Singing...AGAIN! Singer's Edition, p. 30
- Transparency and student copies of 6-1
- Mallet instruments or keyboards

Directions

Display a transparency of 6-1. Help students learn to play the chord roots using bells, keyboard, or other melodic instrument. Select students to play the chord roots as the class sings the song.

Activity 6-2: Choose an Ostinato

Grade Level: 3-4

National Standard: 1

Objective

Students sing ostinatos.

Materials

- Get America Singing...AGAIN! Singer's Edition, p. 30
- Transparency of 6-2

Directions

Display transparency. With students, choose an ostinato to add to the song. Read and rehearse the ostinato. Divide class into two groups, and assign the ostinato to one group and the song to the other. Reverse parts and sing the song again. As time permits, choose another ostinato to add to the song. Add more than one ostinato to create a more complex harmonic texture.

Activity 6-3: Adding Orff

Grade Level: 3-4

National Standard: 2, 4, (5)

Objectives

- Students perform simple instrumental parts while other students sing or play contrasting parts.
- (Optional) Students read traditional notation in 3/4.

Materials

- Get America Singing…AGAIN! Singer's Edition, p. 30
- Teacher copy or transparency of 6-4

Directions

Note transposition to Key of F. Teach instrumental parts to students by reading or by rote. With student input, create an arrangement, layering instrumental parts to create a complex and interesting texture.

Activity 6-4: Add a Countermelody

Grade Level: 3-4

National Standard: 1

Objective

Students sing a countermelody.

Materials

- Get America Singing…AGAIN! Singer's Edition, p. 30
- Student copies of 6-4

Directions

Distribute student copies of 6-4. As students are able to maintain the melody, introduce and rehearse the harmony. Divide the class into two groups. Sing the melody with the harmony part. Allow groups to reverse parts and sing the song again.

Activity 6-5: Study Guide
Grade Level: 5-8
National Standard: 9

Objective
Students understand the origin and background of songs in their varied repertoire.

Materials
- Get America Singing...AGAIN! Singer's Edition, p. 30
- Student copies of 6-5
- Pencils

Directions
Distribute student copies of 6-5. Invite students to read the background information individually or as a class. Divide students into groups. Instruct groups to complete the Vocabulary Builder exercise as instructed on the student page.

Possible student responses: lyrics - the words of a song; canon - composition in which one melody is played or sung in different parts; perish - die; translation - version in another language; original - a new work as opposed to a copy or imitation; Himmel - heaven or sky; Erde - world or earth; die Musika - music; bestehen - remain; bleibet - always.

Activity 6-6: Your Group's Arrangement
Grade Level: 5-8
National Standard: 4

Objective
Students arrange a simple piece for voices or instruments.

Materials
- Get America Singing...AGAIN! Singer's Edition, p 30
- Student copies of 6-6

Directions
Distribute student copies of 6-6. Divide students into groups, and instruct them to follow directions as printed to create an arrangement of the song. Allow time for groups to create and rehearse their arrangements. Invite groups to perform their arrangements for the class. (This activity builds on Activities 6-2, 6-3, 6-4 from earlier grade levels.)

Activity 6-7: Show What You Know

Grade Level: 5-8

National Standard: 9

Objective

Students understand the origin and background of songs in their varied repertoire.

Materials

- Get America Singing…AGAIN! Singer's Edition, p. 30
- Student copies of 6-7
- Pencils

Directions

Distribute student copies of 6-7. Instruct students to work individually, in partners, or in small groups. Encourage students to share their responses with the class. (See "possible student responses" Activity 6-5, p. 72)

Music Alone Shall Live

Playing the Chord Roots

This song uses only three chords. It uses them in a pattern.

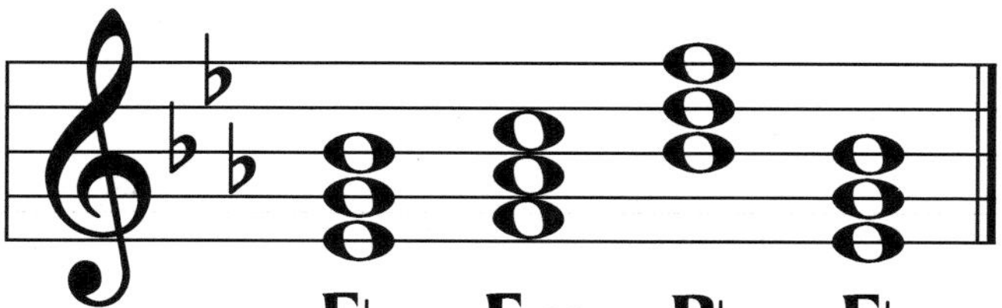

E♭ Fm B♭ E♭

It repeats the pattern three times.

E♭	Fm	B♭	E♭

E♭	Fm	B♭	E♭

E♭	Fm	B♭	E♭

The chords contain these pitches

B♭	C	F	B♭
G	A♭	D	G
E♭	F	B♭	E♭
E♭	Fm	B♭	E♭

Each chord gets its name from the lowest pitch:

the ROOT of the chord.

Play these chord roots. Play them as your class sings the song.

E♭ F B♭ E♭

Music Alone Shall Live

Choose an Ostinato

Ostinato Activity by Loretta Norgon

Ostinato #1

Ostinato #2

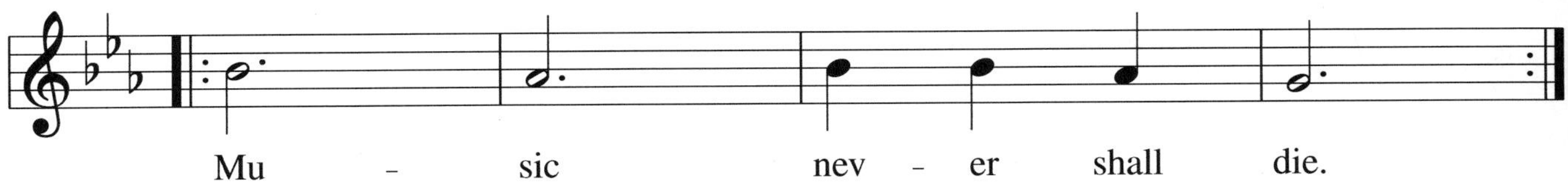

Ostinato #3

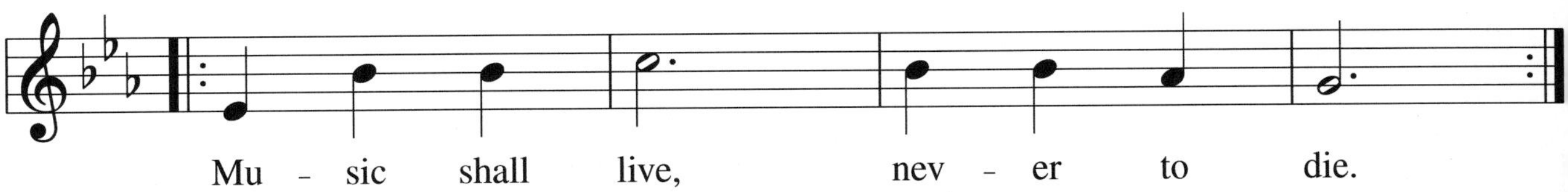

Music Alone Shall Live
Adding Orff

SG = Soprano Glockenspiel
SX = Soprano Xylophone
AX = Alto Xylophone
SR = Soprano Recorder
BX = Bass Xylophone
BM = Bass Metallophone

Traditional
Arranged by Loretta Norgon

Music Alone Shall Live
Add a Countermelody

Traditional German Canon
Countermelody by Loretta Norgon

Music Alone Shall Live

Study Guide

Background Information

The poem, "Music Alone Shall Live" is a translation of "Aber die musika," a canon from Germany. The original lyrics may have been:

Himmel und Erde musen vergehen
Aber die musika
Aber die musika
Aber die musika bleibet bestehen

The most commonly used English translation of the lyrics is:

All things shall perish from under the sky
Music alone shall live
Music alone shall live
Music alone shall live, never to die.

Vocabulary Builder

Can you define these English words?

lyrics canon perish

translation original

Can you define these German words?

Himmel Erde die Musika

bestehen bleibet

Music Alone Shall Live

Your Group's Arrangement

Class: ____________________

Date: ____________________

Group Members: ____

____

Directions: Working as a group, create an arrangement of the song "Music Alone Shall Live."

1. Talk about and make decisions. How you might use:

   English lyrics

   German lyrics

   Instruments

   Harmony

   Introduction and/or coda

   Tempo and dynamics

2. Make a plan. Write or sketch your plan in this space.

3. Try your arrangement. Make changes if needed.

4. Rehearse your arrangement and perform it for your teacher or class.

Music Alone Shall Live

Show What You Know

> All things shall perish from under the sky
> Music alone shall live,
> Music alone shall live,
> Music alone shall live, never to die.

Write your answers to the following questions:

1. What do the lyrics of this song mean?

2. Do you agree with this message? ____Yes ____No
   Why or why not?

3. If you were going to set this poem to music, how would it sound?

4. Choose three of the following Vocabulary Builder words. Write a paragraph including the terms that you choose.

lyrics	canon	perish	translation	original
Himmel	Erde	die Musika	bestehen	

Take Me Out to the Ball Game

Activity 7-1: Reading the Words

Grade Level: 1-2
National Standards: 1

Objective

Students sing a song from memory.

Materials

- Get America Singing...AGAIN! Singer's Edition, p. 43
- Student copies of 7-1: Reading the Words
- Scissors
- Envelopes

Directions

Distribute student copies, scissors, and envelopes. With the class read the lyrics as sequenced on the page. Instruct students to cut the cards apart, shuffle and re-sequence them. When students have their sequences completed, practice reading the lyrics aloud as a class. Sing the song, encouraging students to follow their own lyric card sequences. Distribute envelopes. Encourage students to take their card sets home to share the song with their families.

Activity 7-2: Meter in Threes

Grade Level: 2-4
National Standard: 6

Objective

Students show a triple meter.

Materials

- Get America Singing...AGAIN! Singer's Edition, p. 43
- Transparency and student copies of 7-2

Directions

Display transparency. With students, sing the song and point to the illustrations to demonstrate the strong-weak-weak meter of the song. Distribute student copies of 7-2. As the class sings the song, help students point to the illustrations to identify and feel the meter in threes. Finally, help students create a hand jive that moves in patterns of threes, such as: Pat knees 3X, Clap 3X, Right hand tap chest 3X, Left hand tap chest 3X.

Activity 7-3: About the Song

Grade Level: 3-4

National Standard: 9

Objective

Students understand the origin and background of songs in their varied repertoire.

Materials

- Get America Singing...AGAIN! Singer's Edition, p. 43

Directions

Distribute student copies of 7-3. Invite students to read individually or as a class as appropriate to students' reading abilities. Divide students into groups. Instruct groups to confer, using the "Questions for Discussion." Select a representative from each group to report on the group's discussion and answers to the questions. Assign the research project, setting specific guidelines and parameters as appropriate for the class and students' abilities.

Activity 7-4: Playing the Bass Line

Grade Level: 5-8

National Standard: 2, 5

Objective

Students read and play bass clef notation.

Materials

- Get America Singing...AGAIN! Singer's Edition, p. 43
- Teacher copy or transparency of 7-4
- Mallet instruments, keyboards, or tuned plastic pipes

Directions

Distribute student copies of 7-4. Divide students into four groups. Instruct each group to read and rehearse their portion of the bass line. When groups are ready to perform, sequence the four portions of the bass line. Sing the song while the groups play the bass line. If time permits, allow groups to learn another section of the bass line, and perform the song again.

Activity 7-5: Show What You Know

Grade Level: 5-8

National Standard: 9

Objective

Students understand the origin and background of songs in their varied repertoire.

Materials

- Get America Singing…AGAIN! Singer's Edition, p. 43
- Student copies of 7-5
- Pencils

Directions

Distribute student copies of 7-5. Instruct students to work individually, in partners, or in small groups. Encourage students to share their responses with the class. (This activity builds on Activity 7-3 from earlier grade levels.)

Activity 7-6: Plan Your Own Song

Grade Level: 5-8

National Standard: 4

Objective

Students compose a song within specified guidelines.

Materials

- Student copies of 7-6
- Pencils

Directions

Distribute student copies of 7-6. Invite students to work individually or with partners to plan their compositions as instructed on the student page.

Take Me Out to the Ball Game

Reading the Words

Take me out to the ball game,

Take me out to the crowd.

Buy me some peanuts and cracker-jack.

I don't care if I never get back.

Let me root, root, root for the home team.

If they don't win, it's a shame.

For it's one, two, three strikes,

You're out at the old ball game.

Take Me Out to the Ball Game

Meter in Threes

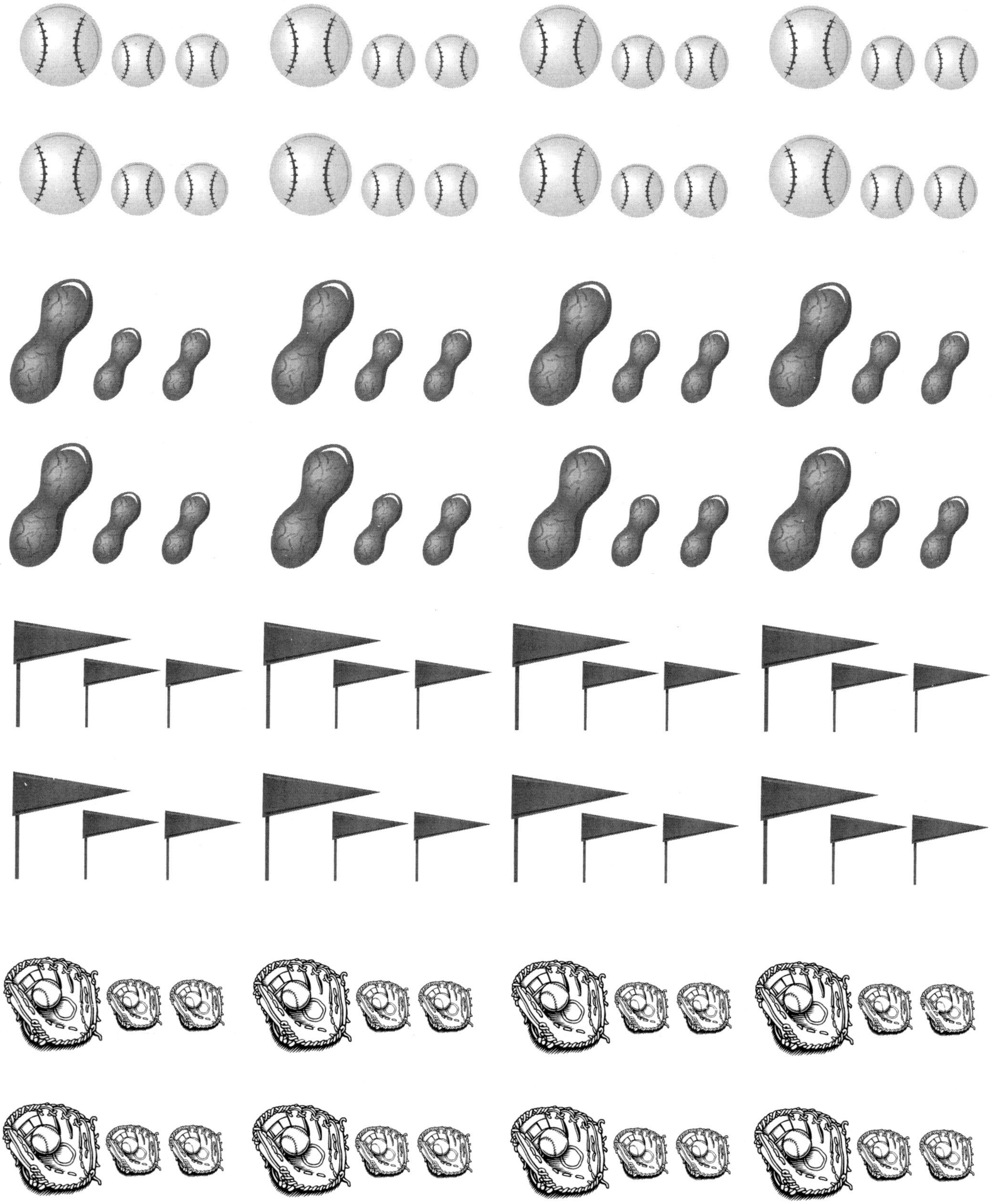

Take Me Out to the Ball Game

About the Song

"Take Me Out to the Ball Game" is sometimes called the anthem of baseball. It is sung at major league games across the country.

Jack Norworth saw a baseball poster while riding on the New York subway in 1908, and, in fifteen minutes, wrote the lyrics for the song. He had never even seen a major league game! In fact, it was 34 years laters, in 1942, that he actually sat in the stands at a major league stadium. A composer named Albert Von Tilzer wrote the music for the song. Like Mr. Norworth, he had not seen a major league game either.

The song gained popularity in the 1949 musical, "Take Me Out to the Ball Game." Harry Caray, the former voice of the Chicago Cubs, made the song part of baseball tradition by singing the chorus with the fans during every seventh-inning stretch.

But the chorus is actually only part of the song. Mr. Norworth also wrote two verses for the song. Verse 1 is about a girl whose boyfriend called and asked her for a date to a show. The girl said, "No, I'd rather go to a ball game." The chorus follows. Verse 2 is also about the girl, how she knew all the players' names, how she argued with the umpire, how she cheered up the fans by singing this song, and, again, leading back to the familiar chorus.

In 1958, on the 50th anniversary of the song, Jack Norworth was presented with a gold lifetime pass to attend major league baseball games. Norworth's original copy of the song is on display at the Baseball Hall of Fame in Cooperstown, New York.

Questions for Discussion

1. What is unusual about the two men who wrote the music and lyrics for this song?
2. Have you known this song for a long time? Do you remember the first time you heard this song?
3. What musical characteristics make this a good song to help baseball fans get in the spirit of a baseball game? (Does it use unity and variety, tension and release, balance, etc.)

Research Assignment

Find more information about this song. Can you find the actual lyrics for the verses? Perhaps you can also find a printed or audio copy of the music for the verses.

Take Me Out to the Ball Game

Playing the Bass Line

Activity by Loretta Norgon

Take Me Out to the Ball Game

Show What You Know

Name______________________________ Class__________ Date________

Write your answers to the following questions:

1. What is the background of the song "Take Me Out to the Ball Game?"

____

____

____

____

2. What did you find interesting about this story?

____

____

____

3. What are the musical and lyrical characteristics that made this song effective?

____

____

____

4. If you were to compose a song for fans at a major sporting event (football, basketball, baseball, hockey, etc.) how would you plan your song?

Lyrics:

Melody:

Harmony/Accompaniment:

Other:

Plan Your Own Song

Choose a Sporting Event

Football	Baseball	Basketball	Hockey
Tennis	Golf	Swimming	Track
Cross Country	Soccer	Cycling	Skiing
__________	__________		

Ideas you want to express:

Your lyrics (First Draft)

Your musical ideas for creating:

- Unity and Variety

- Tension and Release

- Balance

Your lyrics (Revised)

The Star Spangled Banner

Activity 8-1: Learn the Lyrics

Grade Level: 3-4
National Standard: 1

Objective

Students sing a song from memory.

Materials

- Get America Singing…AGAIN! Singer's Edition, p. 44
- Student copies of 8-1
- Pencils

Directions

Open the class period by singing the song. Distribute Singers Editions and student copies of 8-1. Define any unfamiliar words. Invite students to complete the page, working individually, as partners, or as a class as appropriate to students' reading abilities. Challenge students to sing the song from memory.

Activity 8-2: A Closer Look

Grade Level: 3-4
National Standard: 6

Objective

Students respond to prominent musical characteristics while listening to music.

Materials

- Get America Singing…AGAIN! Singer's Edition, p. 44
- Transparency 8-2

Directions

Display transparency. With students, sing the song. Use the transparency to focus students' attention on even/uneven rhythms in the song, and on the melodic contour of key phrases. On a neutral syllable, sing the phrase "And the rocket's red glare." Ask "Which box, #1, #2, #3, or #4, did you hear?" As students identify #3, analyze its melodic and rhythmic content, including the even eighth note pick-up. Continue with the remaining phrase fragments: "Oh, say, can you see," "Whose broad stripes and bright stars," and "O'er the land of the free."

Activity 8-3: Study Guide
Grade Level: 3-4
National Standard: 9

Objective
Students understand the origin and background of songs in their varied repertoire.

Materials
- Get America Singing...AGAIN! Singer's Edition, p. 44
- Student copies of 8-3
- Pencils

Directions
Distribute student copies of 8-3. Invite students to read the background information individually or as a class. Divide students into groups. Instruct groups to complete the Vocabulary Builder exercise as instructed on the student page.

Possible student responses: War of 1812 - War between the United States and Great Britian; Francis Scott Key - American lawyer who wrote the lyrics for "The Star Spangled Banner"; vessel - ship; negotiate - to discuss ways to work toward an agreement between parties; bombardment - an attack with bombs or artillery; Dr. Willam Beanes - friend of Francis Scott Key, held prisoner on a British warship; lyrics - the words of a song; dawn - first appearance of daylight in the morning; twilight - evening, as the sun is just below the horizon; perilous - dangerous; ramparts - barricade; gallantly - bravely; John Stafford Smith - British composer, thought to be the composer of the melody "To Anacreon in Heaven" - used the lyrics of "The Star Spangled Banner"; national anthem - ??

Activity 8-4: Match the Words to the Music
Grade Level: 3-4
National Standard: 2, 5

Objective
Students read traditional notation in 2/4, 3/4, and 4/4 meter signatures.

Materials
- Get America Singing...AGAIN! Singer's Edition, p. 44
- Student copies of 8-4

Directions
Distribute student copies of 8-4. Instruct students to work individually, in partners, or in small groups. Students will read the phrase fragments, sing them aloud, and match the words to each example. Allow time for students to share their answers with the class, and for the class to sing each example. *Answers from p. 91 from top to bottom: 7, 5, 1 (3), 6, 8, 2 (4), 4 (2), 3 (1)*

Activity 8-5: What Is Appropriate?

Grade Level: 3-8
National Standard: 9

Objective

Students understand the origin and background of songs in their varied repertoire.

Materials

- Get America Singing…AGAIN! Singer's Edition, p. 44
- Student copies of 8-5
- Pencils

Directions

Distribute student copies of 8-5. Divide students into groups. Instruct students to discuss each questions and then, individually, write their answers. Facilitate a class discussion in which students share their responses with the class.

Activity 8-6: Transposing

Grade Level: 5-8
National Standard: 6

Objective

Students demonstrate knowledge of the basic principles of tonality, chords, and harmonic progressions in their analyses of music.

Materials

- Student copies of 8-6
- Keyboards or mallet instruments

Directions

Distribute student copies of 8-6. Demonstrate the tonic chord and play the beginning of the song in several keys for the class. Invite students to work individually or in small groups to experiment with transposing as directed on the student page.

Activity 8-7: Key's Article

Grade Level: 5-8

National Standard: 9

Objective

Students understand the origin and background of songs in their varied repertoire.

Materials

- Student copies of 8-7

Directions

Distribute student copies of 8-7. Review the events of the bombardment of Fort McHenry and the origin of our National Anthem (Activity 8-3). Help students begin by making notes and organizing their writing. Instruct students to use the student page (front and back side if necessary) for their rough draft, and to make their final draft of quality that would be accepted by a newspaper office (hand-written or word-processed).

The Star Spangled Banner

Learn the Lyrics

Directions: Fill in the missing words to complete verse one of our National Anthem.

O say, can you see, by the ______________ early ___________,

what so proudly we ___________________ at the

__________________ last _______________________?

Whose broad _______________ and bright stars, through the

_________________ _______________, o'er the ____________

we watched, were so ___________________ streaming?

And the _________________ red glare, the bombs bursting

in air, gave proof through the _________________ that our

_____________ was still there.

O say does that star _________________ _______________

yet wave, o'er the _________________ of the free, and

the ____________________ of the ___________________.

Choose from these words:

dawn's	land
rocket's	hailed
night	perilous
twilight's	flag
light	brave
home	stripes
spangled	gleaming
fight	ramparts
gallantly	banner

The Star Spangled Banner

A Closer Look

1

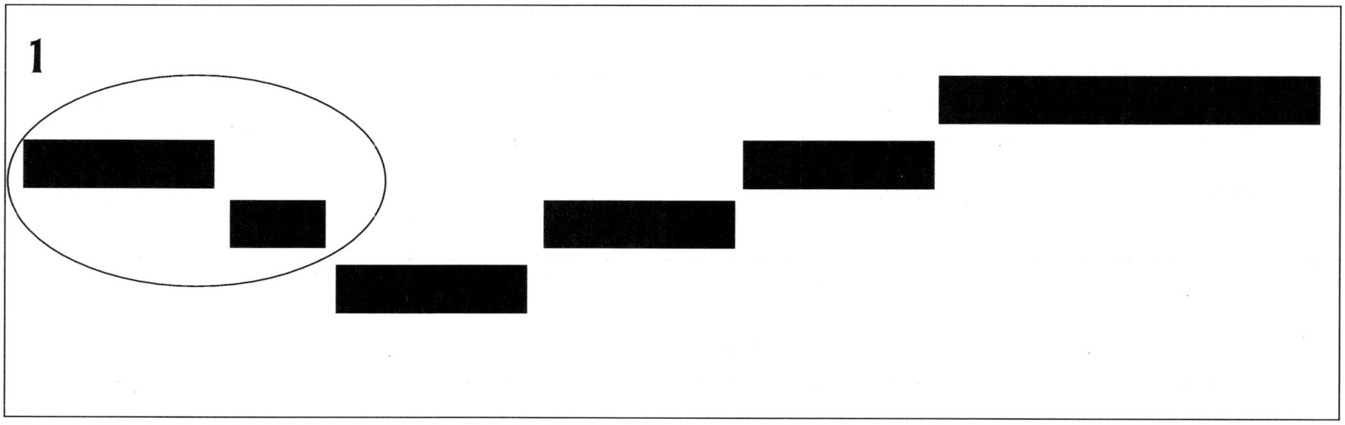

2

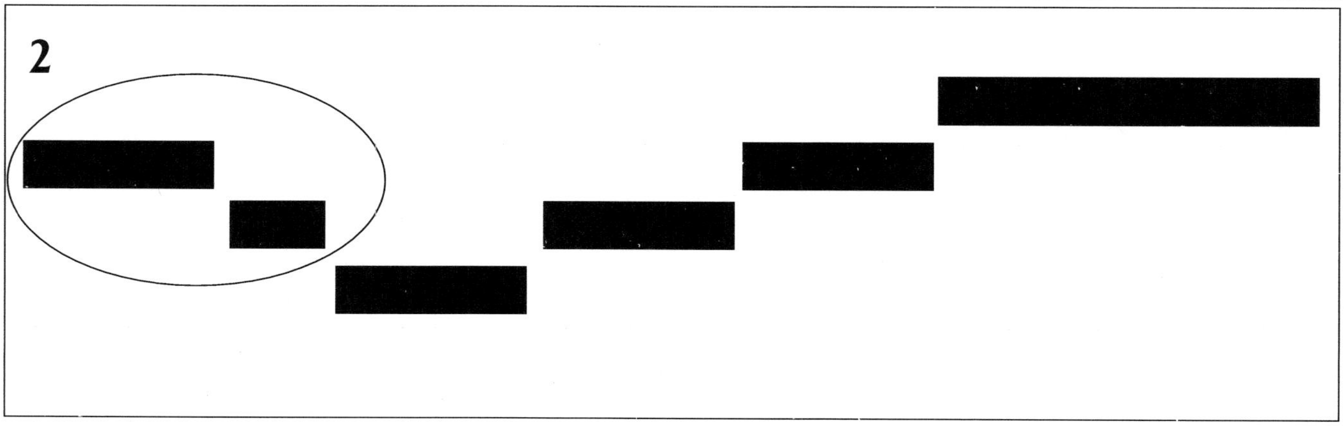

3

4

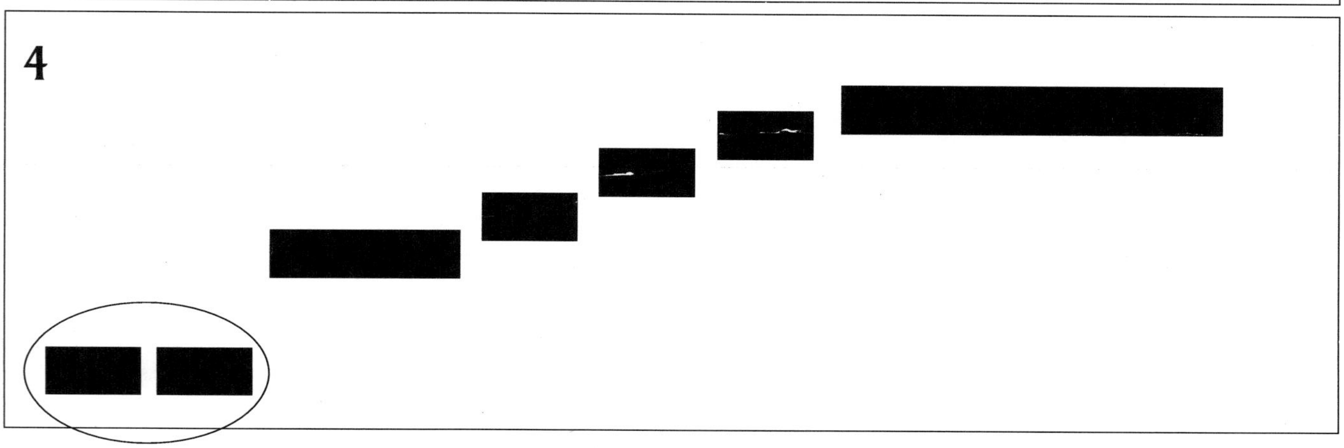

The Star Spangled Banner

Study Guide

Background Information

It was the War of 1812. The British and American forces were battling near Baltimore, near Fort McHenry. Francis Scott Key, a lawyer, was sent to a British warship to help negotiate the release of an American prisoner, Dr. William Beanes. Detained overnight on the vessel, Key witnessed twenty-five hours of the bombardment of Fort McHenry. As the morning sun began to appear over the horizon, he witnessed the stars and strips still waving! Overcome with emotion, he scratched his thoughts and feelings on the back of an envelope.

O say, can you see, by the dawn's early light,
What so proudly we hailed at the twilight's last gleaming?
Whose broad stripes and bright stars, through the perilous fight,
O'er the ramparts we watched were so gallantly streaming?
And the rocket's red glare, the bombs bursting in air,
Gave proof through the night that our flag was still there.
O say, does that Star Spangled Banner yet wave
O'er the land of the free and the home of the brave?

That poem became the lyrics, later to be sung to a popular tune of the times, "To Anachreon in Heaven," probably composed by John Stafford Smith. In 1931, by an act of Congress, "The Star Spangled Banner" became our official national anthem.

Vocabulary Builder

Explain these names, words, and phrases:

War of 1812	Francis Scott Key	vessel	negotiate
bombardment	Dr. William Beanes	lyrics	dawn
twilight	perilous	ramparts	gallantly
John Stafford Smith	national anthem		

The Star Spangled Banner

Match the Words to the Music

1. O say, can you see, ☐

2. What so proudly we hailed ☐

3. Whose broad stripes and bright stars ☐

4. O'er the ramparts we watched ☐

5. And the rocket's red glare ☐

6. Gave proof through the night ☐

7. Oh, say does that star spangled ☐

8. O'er the land of the free ☐

The Star Spangled Banner

What is Appropriate?

Class: ____________________

Date: ____________________

The Flag Code,* adopted by Congress, specifies conduct which is appropriate and acceptable whenever the National Anthem is performed.

> During rendition of the national anthem when the flag is displayed, all present except those in uniform should stand at attention facing the flag with the right hand over the heart. Men not in uniform should remove the headdress with their right hand and hold it at the left shoulder, the hand being over the heart. Persons in uniform should render the military salute at the first note of the anthem and retain this position until the last note. When the flag is not displayed those present should face toward the music and act in the same manner they would if the flag were displayed there.

*Adopted and revised by the National Flag Conference, 1923, 1924
Adopted and revised by Congress, 1942, 1953, 1954, 1968, 1976.

Directions: For each question below, first, discuss with your goup. Then, before going on to the next question, each group member will write his or her own answer.

1. When the National Anthem is played at a public event, what behavior is appropriate?

2. What have you observed at various events during which the National Anthem has been performed?

3. What might have been the reasons that the Flag Code was developed and adopted?

4. What does the National Anthem mean to members of your group?

5. Is there anything that you, personally, will do differently the next time you hear the National Anthem?

The Star Spangled Banner

Transposing

Our country's national anthem begins, using only the four pitches contained in the tonic (I) chord.

1. Play these pitches as you sing the beginning of this song.

The pitches (in Key of A♭)

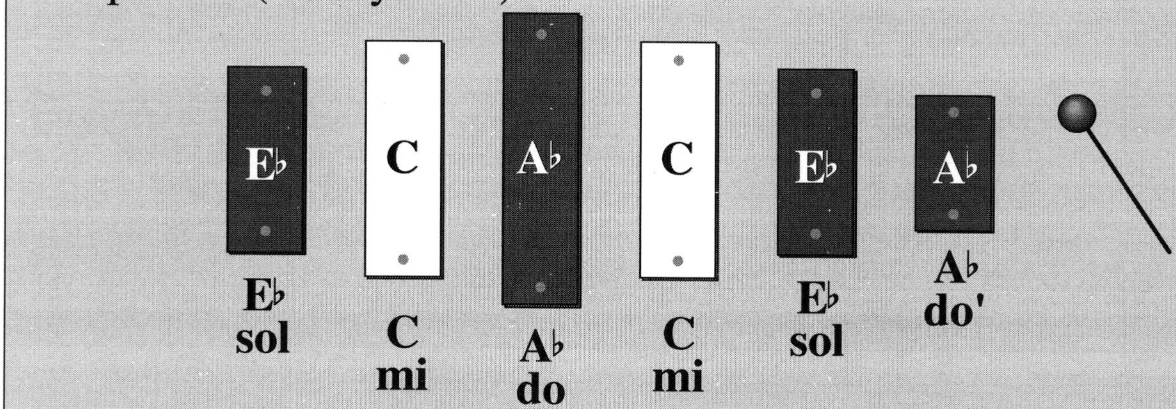

2. Transpose the pitches for the tonic chord and play the beginning of this song in the key of B♭

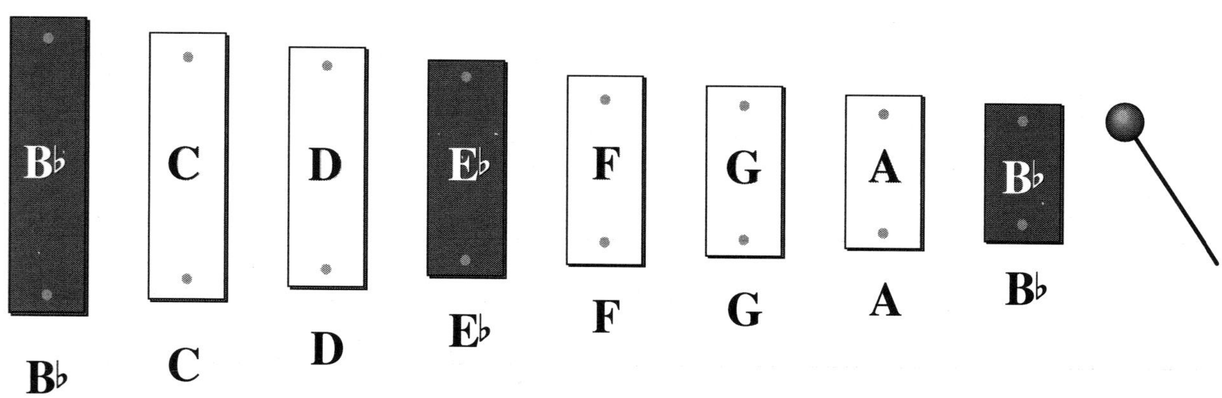

3. Transpose the beginning of this song into other keys.

The Star Spangled Banner

Key's Article

The Assignment: You are Francis Scott Key. You've been asked to write an article for the local newspaper describing your experience and ordeal aboard the British warship, and your reasons for writing your poem, "The Star Spangled Banner."

Your notes or outline:

First Draft

Teacher Instructions

Zip-A-Dee-Doo-Dah

Activity 9-1: Find Parts that Match

Grade Level: K-2

National Standard: 1

Objective

Students sing a song from memory.

Materials

- Get America Singing...AGAIN! Singer's Edition, p. 46
- Transparency and student copies of 9-1
- Plastic counting chips

Directions

Open the class period by singing the song. Display transparency. Sing the song pointing out each phrase on the map as the class sings. Sing one of the phrases on a neutral syllable. Ask "Which part did you hear?" Allow students to identify phrases from the song as they hear them. Distribute student copies of 9-1 and one chip for each student. Sing a phrase and instruct students to place the chip to identity the section that they hear. Conclude the class period by singing the entire song one more time.

Activity 9-2: Home Tone

Grade Level: 1-2

National Standard: 6

Objective

Students respond to prominent musical characteristics while listening to music.

Materials

- Get America Singing...AGAIN! Singer's Edition, p. 46
- Transparency 9-2
- B flat resonator bell

Directions

Display transparency. With students, sing the song. Use the transparency to focus students' attention on the ending pitch of each phrase or phrase fragment. For each fragment, help students check the ending pitch with the B flat bell. If the pitches match, place an X in the house (houses #4 and #8). As you complete the page, focus a discussion on the significance of the home tone.

Activities 9-3: Loud and Soft (Grades 1-2)
9-4: Dynamics: Italian Terms (Grades 3-4)
9-5: Planner Page

Grade Level: 1-4

National Standard: 5

Objective

Students identify and interpret dynamic symbols.

Materials

- Get America Singing...AGAIN! Singer's Edition, p. 46
- Transparencies and student copies of 9-3, 9-4, 9-5
- Pencils

Directions

Display transparency of 9-3 or 9-4. Introduce or reinforce dynamic terms. Display transparency of 9-5, the planner page. Help students plan a performance of the song, marking the transparency with dynamic symbols. Perform, evaluate, and revise as needed.

Activity 9-6: Our Group's Arrangement

Grade Level: 5-8

National Standard: 4

Objective

Students arrange a simple piece for voices or instruments.

Materials

- Get America Singing...AGAIN! Singer's Edition, p. 46
- Student copies of 9-6

Directions

Distribute student copies of 9-6. Divide students into groups, and instruct them to follow directions as printed to create an arrangement of the song. Allow time for groups to create and practice their arrangements. Invite groups to perform their arrangements for the teacher or for the class.

Activity 9-7: An Oscar-Winning Song

Grade Level: 5-8

National Standard: 9

Objective

Students understand the origin and background of songs in their varied repertoire.

Materials

- Get America Singing…AGAIN! Singer's Edition, p. 46
- Student copies of 9-7
- Pencils

Directions

Distribute student copies of 9-7. Invite students to read the background information individually or as a class. Discuss the suggested research projects. Encourage students to suggest other ideas to continue their study of the song and the musical. Assign research projects for individuals, partners, or groups, along with specific requirements of the assignment.

Answers: Walt Disney - owner of Disney Studios who produced the movie *Song of the South*; Joel Chandler Harris - collector of folk tales, among them *The Complete Tales of Uncle Remus*; Bobby Driscol - starred as "Johnny" in *Song of the South*; Ruth Warrick - starred as "Sally" in *Song of the South*; James Baskett - starred as "Uncle Remus" in Song of the South; Charles Wolcott - music director for *Song of the South*

Activity 9-8: Show What You Know

Grade Level: 5-8

National Standard: 9

Objective

Students understand the origin and background of songs in their varied repertoire.

Materials

- Get America Singing…AGAIN! Singer's Edition, p. 46
- Student copies of 9-8
- Pencils

Directions

Distribute student copies of 9-8. Instruct students to work individually, in partners, or in small groups. Encourage students to share their responses with the class.

Zip-A-Dee-Doo-Dah

Find Parts that Match

1 Zip 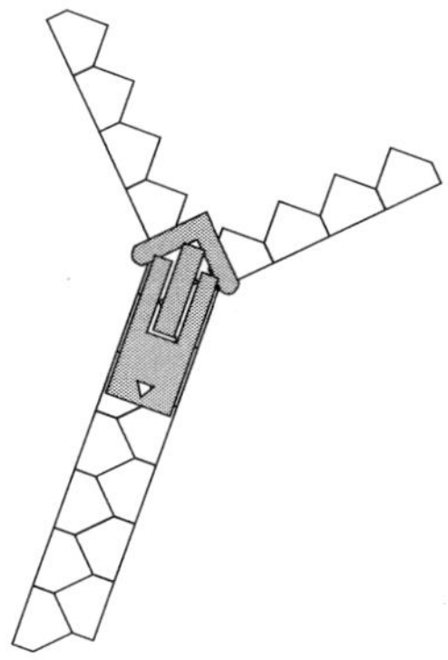	2 My
3 	4 Zip 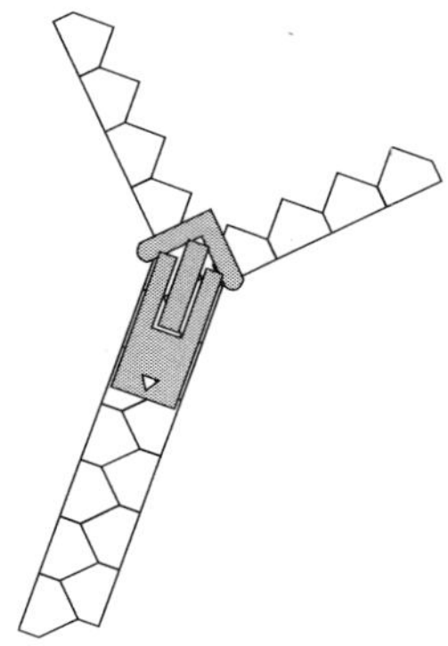
5 	6 truth
7 Zip 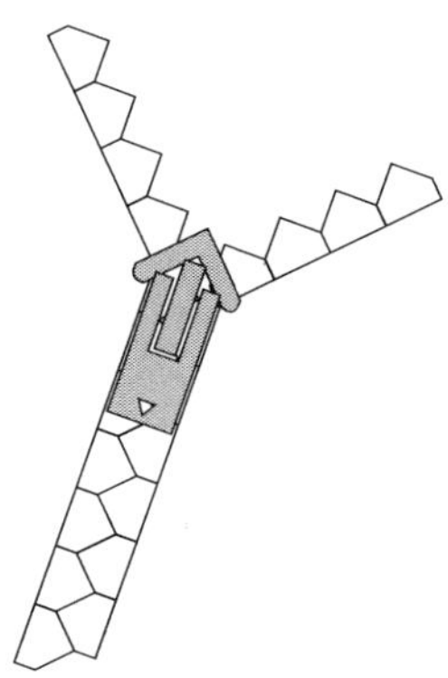	8 

Zip-A-Dee-Doo-Dah

Home Tone

1

Zip

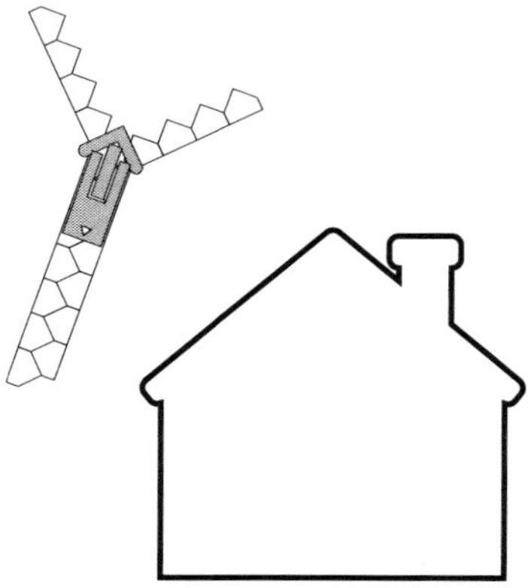

2

My

3

4

Zip

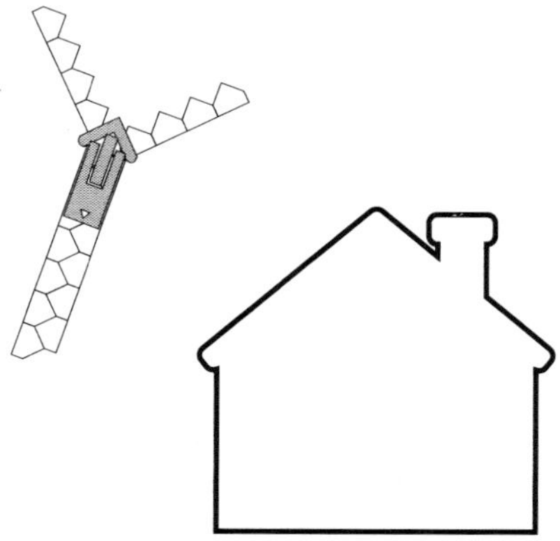

5

6

truth

7

Zip

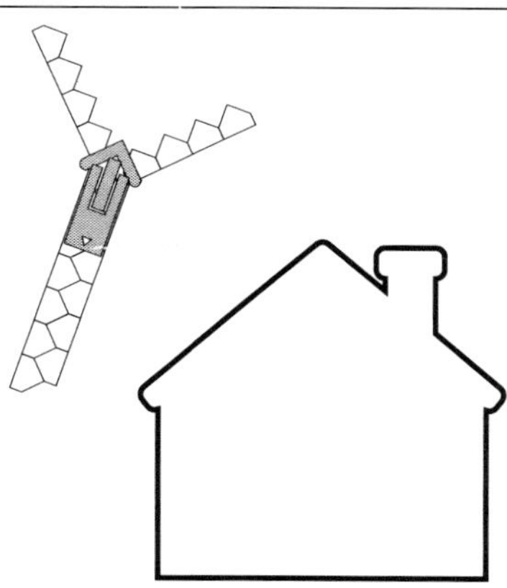

8

Zip-A-Dee-Doo-Dah

Loud and Soft

<table>
<tr><td>p</td><td>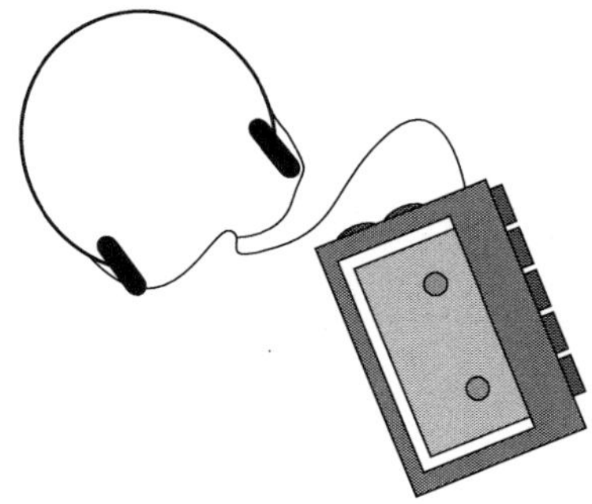</td><td>soft</td></tr>
<tr><td>f</td><td></td><td>loud</td></tr>
<tr><td>ff</td><td></td><td>very loud</td></tr>
</table>

Zip-A-Dee-Doo-Dah

Dynamics – Italian Terms

pp	pianissimo	very soft
p	piano	soft
mp	mezzo piano	medium soft
mf	mezzo forte	medium loud
f	forte	loud
ff	fortissimo	very loud
$>$	decrescendo	getting softer
$<$	crescendo	getting louder

Zip-A-Dee-Doo-Dah

Planner Page

1 Zip 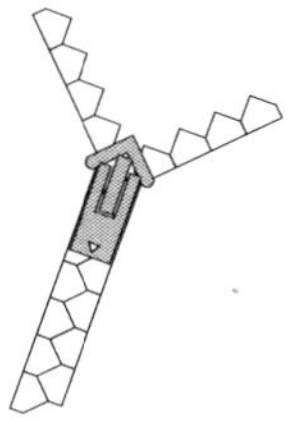	**2** My
3 	**4** Zip 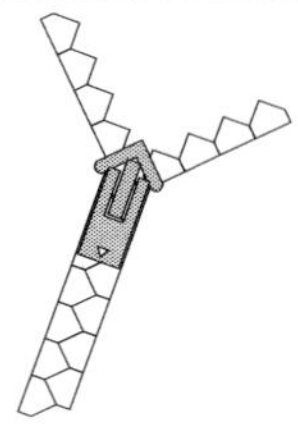
5 	**6** truth
7 Zip 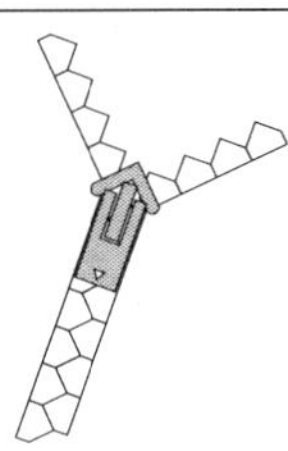	**8** 

Zip-A-Dee-Doo-Dah

Our Group's Arrangement

Class: ____________________

Date: ____________________

Group Members ____

Ideas for Singing	Ideas for Playing	Other Ideas
____________	____________	____________
____________	____________	____________
____________	____________	____________
____________	____________	____________

Decisions to Make

Introduction "Get ready" music ____________________

Coda - Ending music ____________________

Interlude(s) - between sections ____________________

Repeats - how many times? ____________________

Who will sing and when? ____________________

Who will play and when? ____________________

What instruments will you use? ____________________

Accompaniment ____________________

Tempo ____________________

Dynamics ____________________

Other: ____________________

Our Plan

____

____

____

____

____

____

____

____

____

____

____

Zip-A-Dee-Doo-Dah

An Oscar-Winning Song

Background Information

"Zip-A-Dee-Doo-Dah" was introduced in the Disney movie, *Song of the South*. The lyrics were written by Ray Gilbert, and the music was composed by Allie Wrubel. "Zip-A-Dee-Doo-Dah" won the Best Song Oscar for 1947. The song was recorded and popularized by Johnny Mercer and The Pied Pipers.

Released in 1946, *Song of the South* used a combination of live actors and animated characters. James Baskett won an Honorary Oscar Award for his performance as Uncle Remus. In addition to Uncle Remus, movie characters included Johnny, Ginny, Br'er Fox, Br'er Bear, and Br'er Rabbit.

Other songs from the movie included:
"Uncle Remus Said"
"How Do You Do?"
"Ev'rybody's Got a Laughing Place"

Research Projects

1. Who were the following, and what were their connections to the movie, *Song of the South.*

   Walt Disney — Joel Chandler Harris — Bobby Driscoll
   Ruth Warrick — James Baskett — Charles Wolcott

2. Can you find a recording of "Zip-A-Dee-Doo-Dah" performed by Johnny Mercer and The Pied Pipers?

3. Can your find a recording or printed version of one of the other songs from the movie?

4. What other Disney movies have combined live actors and animation? Explain the process used.

5. What other Disney songs have won Oscars?

Zip-A-Dee-Doo-Dah

Show What You Know

Name______________________________ Class__________ Date________

Write your answers to the following questions:

1. Explain the origin of this song.

____

____

____

2. What do you like about this song?
   Explain your answer using musical terms.

____

____

____

____

____

____

3. Write a paragraph using at least three of the following names, words or phrases.

Walt Disney	Uncle Remus	Oscar for Best Song
Song of the South	Br'er Rabbit	animation
lyrics	Gilbert & Wrubel	

____

____

____

____

____

____

____

____

____

____

____

____

Teacher Instructions

This Little Light of Mine

Activity 10-1: Stair Stepping

Grade Level: K-2
National Standard: 5

Objective

Students use a system (syllables) to read simple pitch notation.

Materials

- Get America Singing...AGAIN! Singer's Edition, p. 47
- Transparency and student copies of 10-1

Directions

Open the class period by singing the song. Focus on the ending. Display transparency. Sing the song pointing out stair steps on the map as the class sings. Discuss the melodic contour represented by the steps. Practice the hand signs and incorporate as you sing the song again. Distribute student copies of 10-1, and invite students to point to the steps as they sing the song. Encourage students to take the pages home and perform the song for their families.

Activity 10-2: Let It Shine

Grade Level: 1-2
National Standard: 2, 6

Objective

Students add instruments and movement to a song.

Materials

- Get America Singing...AGAIN! Singer's Edition, p. 47
- Transparency of 10-2
- Resonator bells, classroom percussion instruments

Directions

Display transparency. With students, sing the song. Use the transparency to focus students' attention on the ending pitch of each occurrence of "let it shine," at the end of the song. For each "Let it shine," help students play the ending pitch. Next focus on the "Instrument" boxes. Encourage students to select a classroom instrument (e.g., triangle, finger cymbals, wind chimes) to play as they sing the word "shine." Use the boxes to record the class' choice, either with a picture or by writing the name of the instrument in the box. Finally, encourage students to suggest ways that they could incorporate body movement into the song, adding a movement each time they sing the words "Let it shine." Record the movement suggestions in the "Movement" boxes, and perform the entire song.

Activity 10-3: Play Along

Grade Level: 1-2

National Standard: 2

Objective

Students perform easy melodic patterns accurately and independently on classroom instruments.

Materials

- Get America Singing...AGAIN! Singer's Edition, p. 47
- Transparency and Student copies of 10-3
- Resonator bells

Directions

Display the transparency or distribute student copies of 10-3. Help students read the melodic contour and match it to the song. Select individual students to play the melody fragments on bells. Sing the song with the class. Invite individuals to play along.

Activity 10-4: Learn the Signs

Grade Level: K-4

National Standard: 8

Objective

Students perform a song with signs.

Materials

- Get America Singing...AGAIN! Singer's Edition, p. 47
- Transparency and Student copies of 10-4

Directions

Display the transparency. Introduce and demonstrate signs, one at a time. Allow time for students to practice each sign, reviewing and incorporating the previously learned signs as new ones are added. Perform the song with the signs.

Activity 10-5: Accompany the Song

Grade Level: 3-4

National Standard: 2

Objective

Students perform easy chordal patterns accurately on classroom harmonic instruments.

Materials

- Get America Singing…AGAIN! Singer's Edition, p. 47
- Transparency of 10-5
- bells, handbells, tuned pipes, tuned water glasses, guitar, or other instruments

Directions

Display transparency of 10-5. Distribute instruments. Rehearse the chordal accompaniment. Sing the song with the accompaniment.

Activity 10-6: Arrange the Cards

Grade Level: 3-4

National Standard: 5

Objective

Students read rhythm and pitch notation.

Materials

- Get America Singing…AGAIN! Singer's Edition, p. 47
- Student copies of 10-6
- Scissors

Directions

Divide class into small groups. Distribute one student copy of 10-6 and a pair of scissors to each group. Instruct students to cut the cards apart, shuffle them, read the melodies, and put the cards in the correct order to match the song. Encourage students to share their answers with the class. When all groups have the sequence correct, sing the song.

Activity 10-7: Partner Songs

Grade Level: 3-4

National Standard: 1

Objective

Students sing partner songs.

Materials

- Get America Singing…AGAIN! Singer's Edition, p. 47
- Student copies of 10-7

Directions

Note transposition to Key of F Major. Distribute student copies of 10-7. As students are able to maintain the melody, introduce and rehearse the partner song. Divide the class into two groups. Sing the melody with the partner song. Allow groups to reverse parts and sing the song again.

Activity 10-8: Recorder Harmony

Grade Level: 5-8

National Standard: 2

Objective

Students play a recorder duet.

Materials

- Get America Singing…AGAIN! Singer's Edition, p. 47
- Student copies of 10-8
- Recorders

Directions

Distribute student copies of 10-8. Divide class into two groups. Assist one group in learning the melody. Assist the other group in learning to play the harmony part. Pair each student with a partner and allow time for the partners to rehearse their duets. Encourage duets to perform for the class. Reassemble the groups, and work with each group to help them learn the opposite part. Pair with partners again, allow time for practice, and performances.

Activity 10-9: Study Guide

Grade Level: 5-8

National Standard: 9

Objective

Students understand the origin and background of songs in their varied repertoire.

Materials

- Get America Singing…AGAIN! Singer's Edition, p. 47
- Student copies of 10-9
- Pencils

Directions

Distribute student copies of 10-9. Instruct students to work individually, in partners, or in small groups. Encourage students to share their responses with the class.

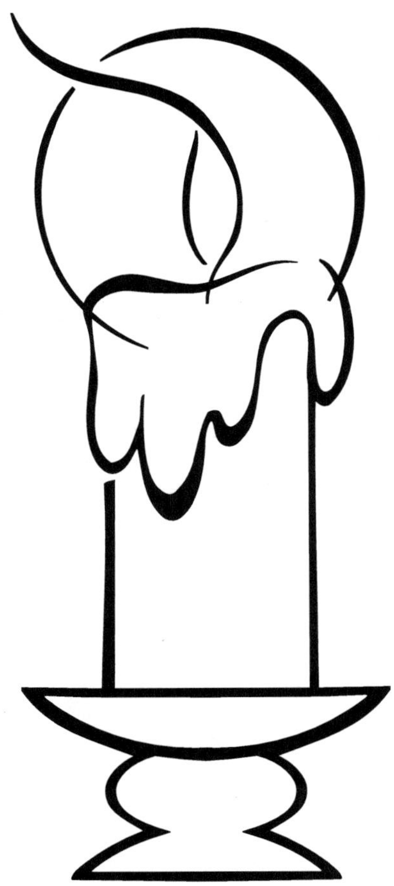

This Little Light of Mine

Stair Stepping

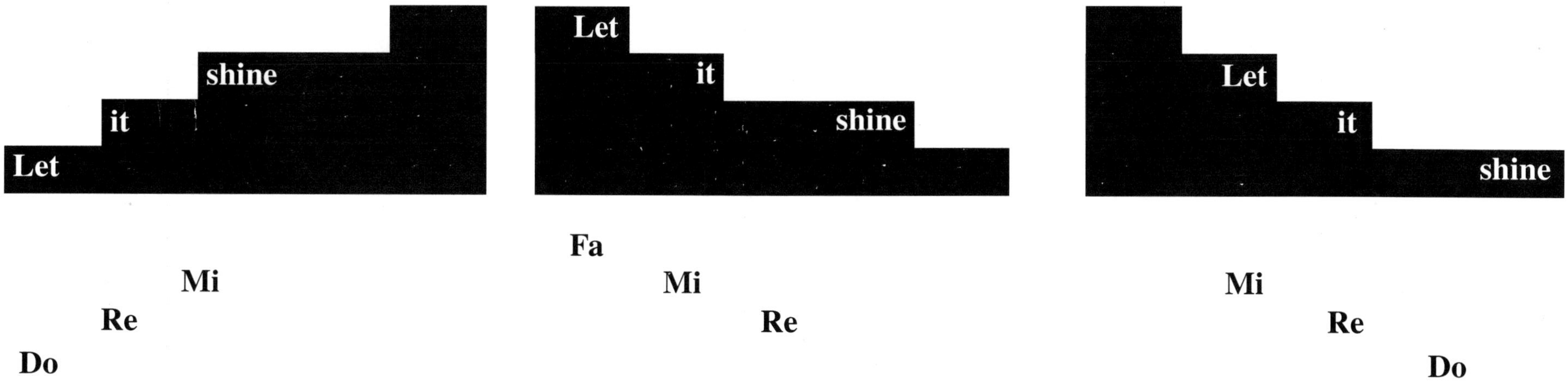

Do you know the hand signs?

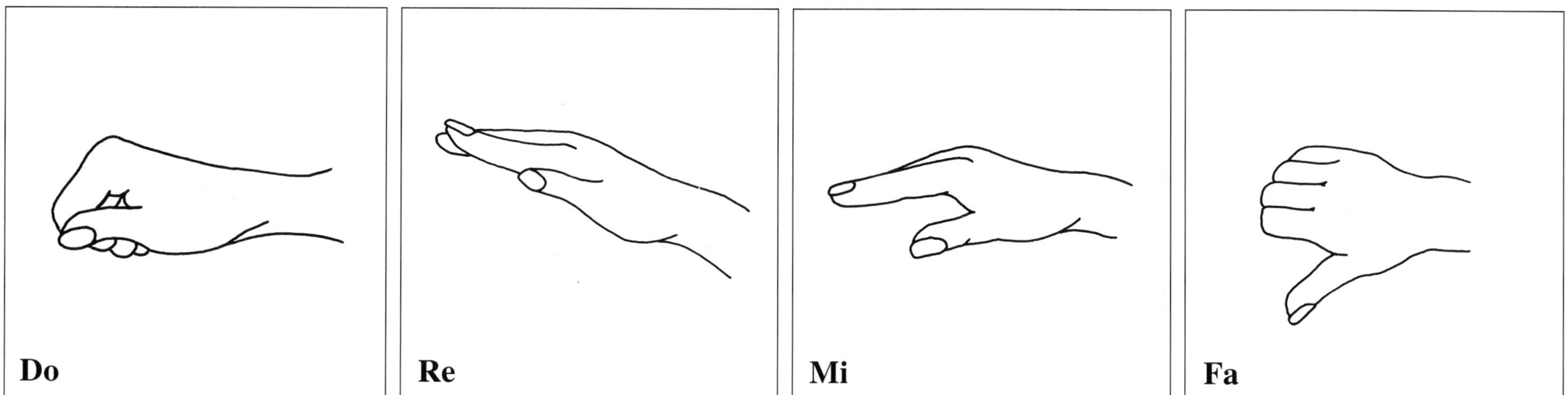

This Little Light of Mine

Let It Shine

	Instrument	Movement
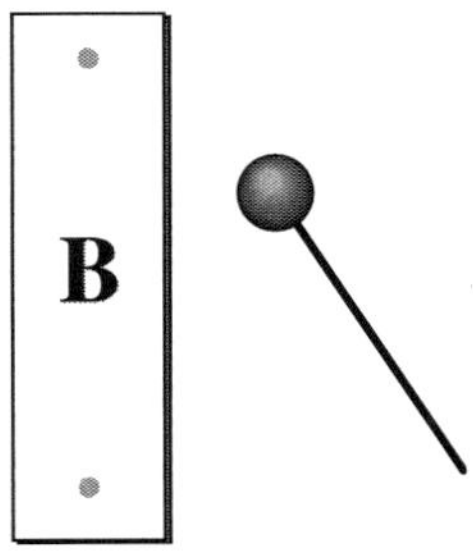 Let it shine		
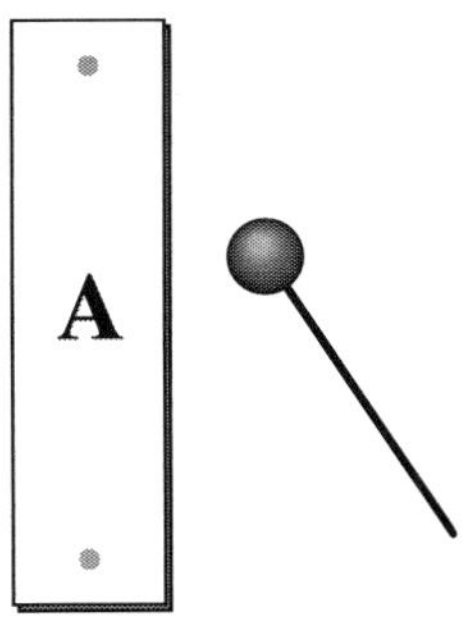 Let it shine		
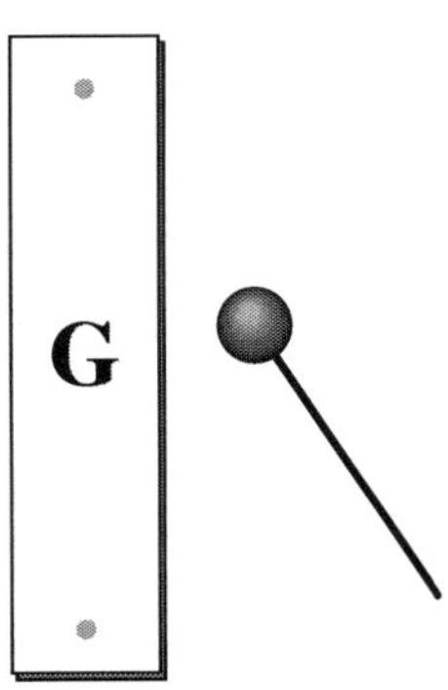 Let it shine		

This Little Light of Mine

Play Along

Find these bells. Play along with the song.

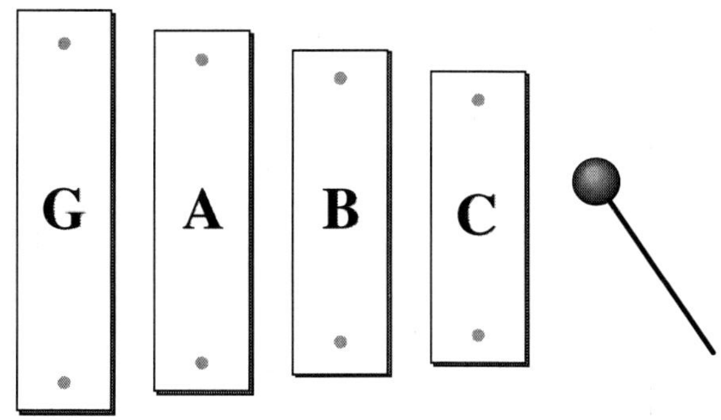

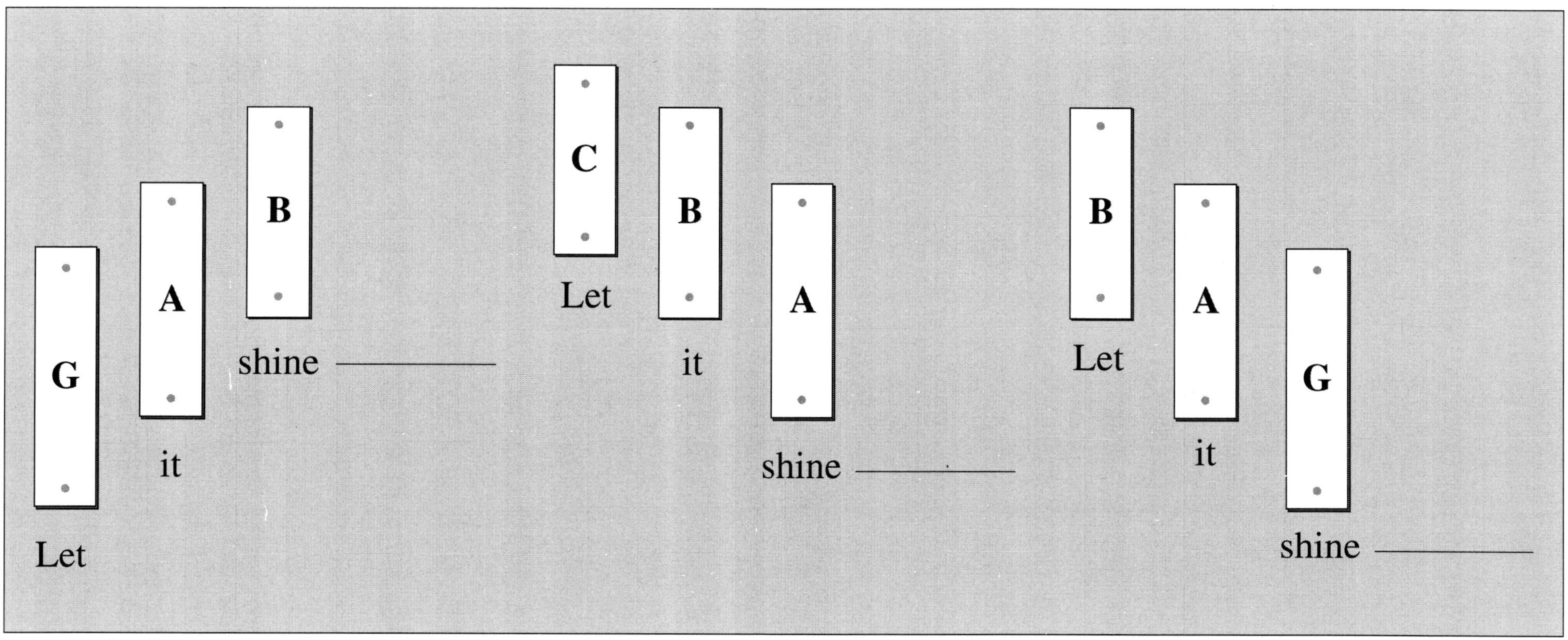

This Little Light of Mine

Learn the Signs

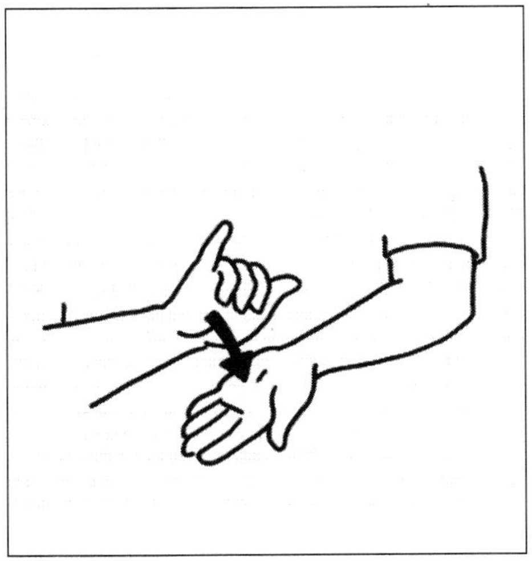

This

little

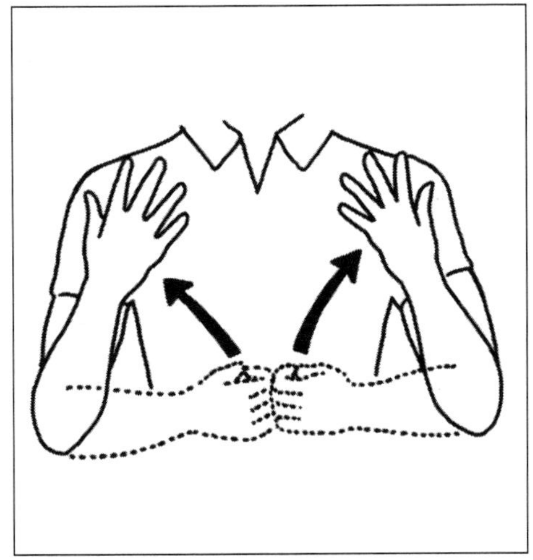

light

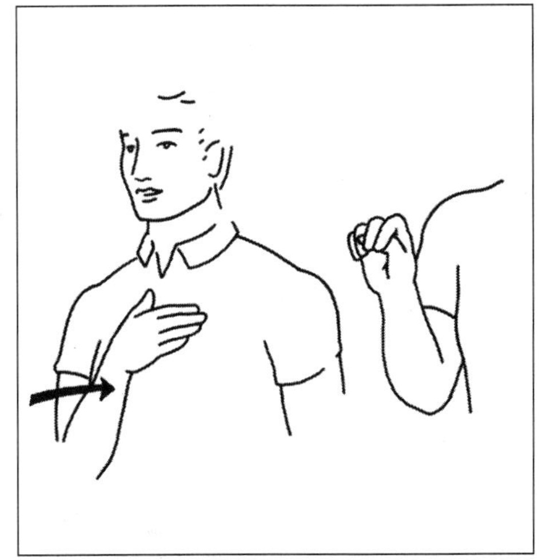

mine

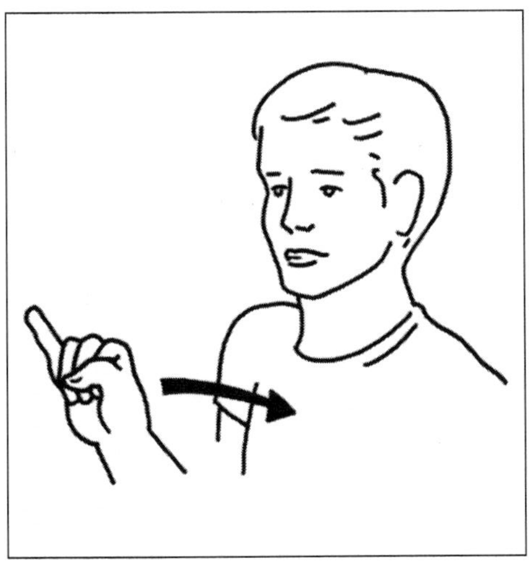

I

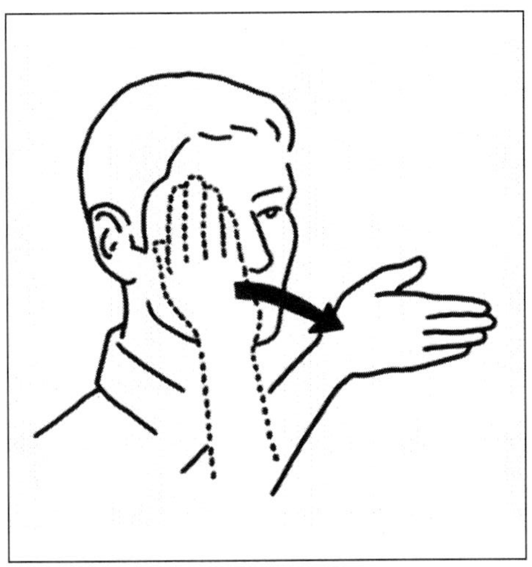

will

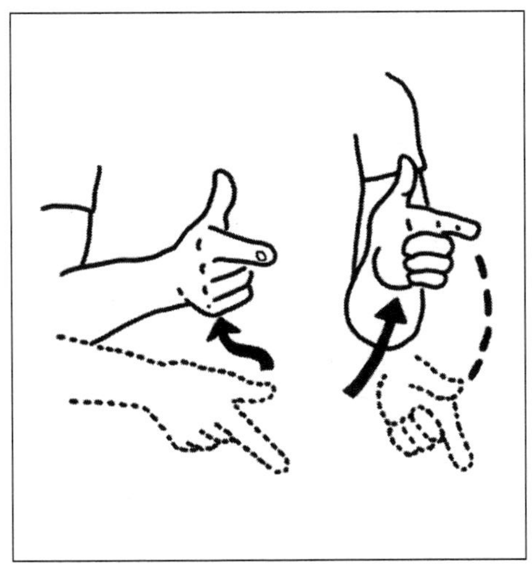

let

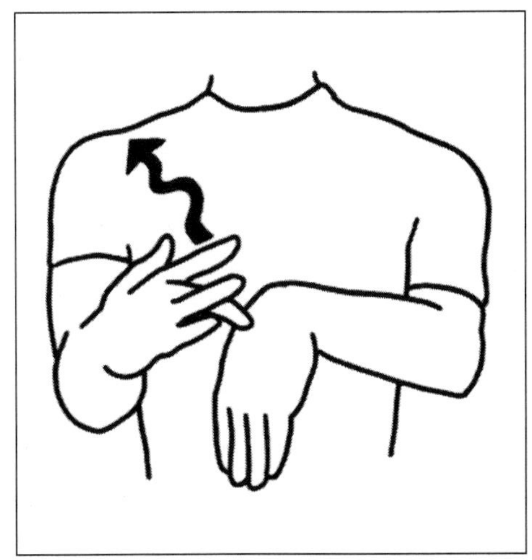

shine

This Little Light of Mine

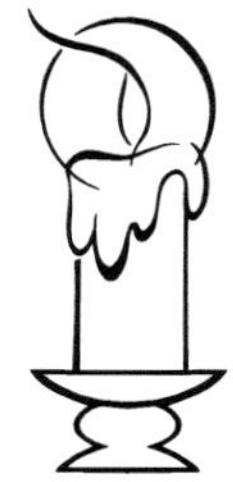

Accompany the Song

Directions: Using bells, handbells, tuned pipes, tuned water glasses, guitar, or other instruments, sing, and accompany "This Little Light of Mine." The song uses these chords.

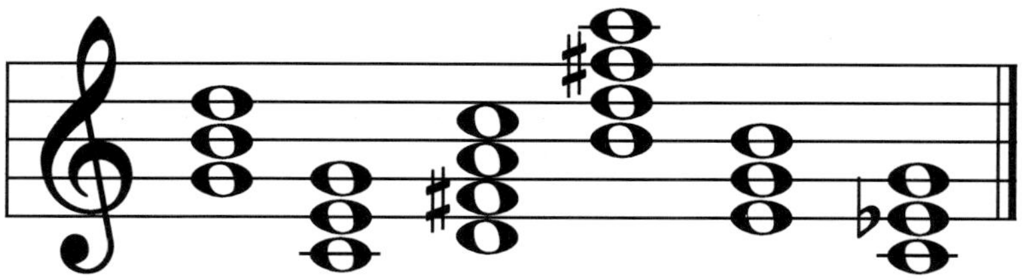

G C D7 B7 Em Cm

G Chord	C Chord	D7 Chord	B7 Chord	Em Chord	Cm Chord
G B D	C E G	D F♯ A C	B D♯ F♯ A	E G B	C E♭ G

(D B G) This little light of mine, ___________ (C A F♯ D) I'm gonna let it shine. (D B G) ___________

(G E C) This little light of mine, ___________ I'm gonna let it shine. (D B G) ___________

(D B G) This little light of mine, ___________ (A F♯ D♯ B) I'm gonna let it shine. (B G E) ___________

(G E♭ C) Let it shine, (D B G) ___________ Let it shine, (C A F♯ D) ___________ Let it shine. (D B G) (G E C) (D B G) ___________

This Little Light of Mine

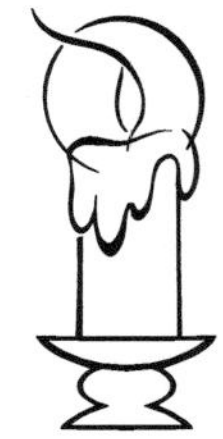

Arrange the Cards

Directions: Cut these cards apart and shuffle them. Then, one-by-one, read the melodies and put the cards in the correct order to match the song "This Little Light of Mine."

This Little Light of Mine

Partner Songs

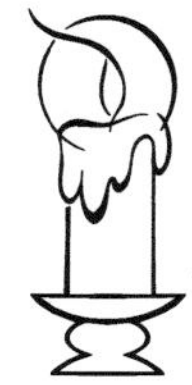

Traditional
Partner Song by Loretta Norgon

This Little Light of Mine

Recorder Harmony

Recorder Part by Loretta Norgon

This Little Light of Mine

Study Guide

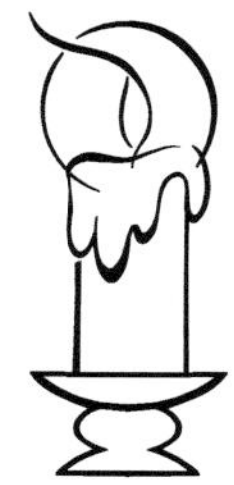

Background Information

Slaves, who were brought to the United States from West Africa, expressed their deep feelings through worship songs and work songs. By combining African vocal techniques with church humns of the white people, a whole new type of musc – the spiritual – was born.

Spirituals showed a direct connection to African roots through vocal slides, slurs, raised and lowered pitches and variations in rhythm. Lyrics of spirituals expressed high emotion. But, in spite of troubled lives, the spirituals spoke of hope and faith—something better to come. The lyrics of "This Little Light of Mine," used "light" as a symbol of hope.

Spirituals were sung without accompaniment. Singers improvised to express their joys and sorrows. Music united the singers and gave them power. Call and response featured a lead singer with members of the group responding as they maintained a strong steady beat. Singers were encouraged to improvise, often with clapping and stamping to maintain the steady beat.

Spirituals provided the roots for blues and jazz—both to come later.

Vocabulary Builder

Can you define these words and phrases?

slaves	West Africa	spiritual
slides	call and response	slurs
symbol of hope	improvising	accompaniment
steady beat	blues	jazz

The National Standards

1. Singing, alone and with others, a varied repertoire of music

2. Performing on instruments, alone and with others, a varied repertoire of music

3. Improvising melodies, variations, and accompaniments

4. Composing and arranging music within specified guidelines

5. Reading and notating music

6. Listening to, analyzing, and describing music

7. Evaluating music and music performances

8. Understanding relationships between music, the other arts, and disciplines outside the arts

9. Understanding music in relation to history and culture

About the Author

Loretta Mitchell Norgon serves as a classroom music coordinator K-8 for the Brainerd, Minnesota Public Schools. She also coordinates the Beginning Teacher Support System, a formal induction program to support, assess, and improve the performance and effectiveness of beginning teachers. She earned the B.A. summa cum laude from St. Olaf College with a major in music education, and the M.S. as a graduate fellow in music education from the University of Illinois.

Under her leadership, Brainerd's classroom music department has been recognized as an exemplary model of standards-based education, and was awarded the Minnesota Alliance for Arts in Education Program of Excellence Award. The department's instructional materials, aligned with the National Standards for Music Education, as well as the department's website address, are requested and shared with music educators across the country.

Mrs. Norgon is sought after as a presenter for seminars and workshops for regional, state and national education conferences. Active in professional organizations, her positions have included Classroom Music Vice President of Minnesota Music Educators Association and President of Minnesota Elementary Music Educators K-8. She teaches off-campus graduate level courses for music specialists and professional development courses for teachers of all disciplines Pre-K-12.

Throughout her teaching career, she has participated in strategic planning and development groups. She has served on the Commissioner's Task Force for Restructuring Education, the Minnesota Graduation Rules Change Committee, the Committee for Outcome Based Education in Music, the development task force, the Minnesota Handbook for Music Education review team, trainer and lead scorer for the Minnesota music assessment scoring team, trainer in Professional Development Planning for teachers and Education Minnesota's "Teachers as Leaders and Learners" Project.

In addition to *Get America Singing Again - Strategies for Teaching (Set A)*, Mrs. Norgon is the author of six other music education resources, and a contributing author for a seventh publication, the *Primary Teacher's Ready-to-Use Activity Program* (Parker/Prentice Hall, 1989). Her original approach to teaching music reading became the foundation for the *Ready-to-Use Music Reading Activities Kit*, published by Parker/Prentice Hall in 1991. Her other publications include *One, Two, Three...Echo Me!*, (1991), and the *Music Teacher's Almanac* (1992), published by Parker/Prentice Hall; and *101 Bulletin Boards for the Music Classroom* (1989), *Bulletin Boards that Teach Music* (1995), and *Above and Beyond* (1999), all published by Hal Leonard Corporation. She is also a regular columnist and contributor to *Music Express!*, a bi-monthly publication for general music teachers, published by Cherry Lane Magazines.